ALSO BY ALFRED APPEL, JR.

The Annotated Lolita

Nabokov's Dark Cinema

Signs of Life

EDITED BY:

Witching Times

Nabokov

The Bitter Air of Exile: Russian Writers in the West, 1922–1972

The Art of Celebration

The Art of Celebration

Twentieth-Century Painting, Literature,
Sculpture, Photography, and Jazz

Alfred Appel, Jr.

Alfred A. Knopf, Inc.   *New York*   *1992*

A NOTE ON THE TYPE

This book was set in a digitized version of Janson. The hot-metal version of Janson was a recutting made direct from type cast from matrices long thought to have been made by the Dutchman Anton Janson, who was a practicing type founder in Leipzig during the years 1668–1687. However, it has been conclusively demonstrated that these types are actually the work of Nicholas Kis (1650-1702), a Hungarian, who most probably learned his trade from the master Dutch type founder Dirk Voskens. The type is an excellent example of the influential and sturdy Dutch types that prevailed in England up to the time William Caslon (1692–1766) developed his own incomparable designs from them.

Composed by Graphic Composition, Inc., Athens, Georgia
Separations by Accent on Color, Hauppauge, New York
Halftones by Halliday Lithographers, Inc.,
West Hanover, Massachusetts
Printed and bound by Worzalla Printers,
Stevens Point, Wisconsin
Designed by Mia Vander Els

Frontispiece: Alexander Calder, *Gibraltar*, 1936.

To my grandchildren,

STEPHEN EDWARD OSHMAN *and*

KATHERINE CLAIRE OSHMAN

Contents

The Art of Celebration

Alexander Calder, *Thirteen Spines*, 1940. Photograph by Herbert Matter.

Female Idol (front and rear view), Turkey, Neolithic period,
c. 5600 B.C. Polished terra cotta. Such fertility amulets were small enough to
carry on one's person at all times (about three inches long, one inch wide).

The City Meets the Country

AFTER SEVERAL DECADES on a pedestal in the outdoor sculpture garden of New York's Museum of Modern Art, Gaston Lachaise's bronze *Floating Figure* (1927) has been moved indoors, to an even more commanding position at the head of the only stairway leading to the Permanent Collection on the second floor (opposite). *Floating Figure*'s signal position in the world's greatest modern art museum is paradoxical, inasmuch as its representational form draws on archaic sources and is as perfectly poised as any classical work, which is hardly in keeping with the public's sense of modernism in the arts: that it is unfathomably abstract and obscure, dispiriting and depressing, especially in literature. This book intends to correct this tired half-truth by urging that we properly appreciate an enriching body of work that can be called "celebratory modernism," and that we do so before the works in question have grown even dimmer or have disappeared entirely behind the newest academic fog banks.

The polarities of modernism — and, one might say, of human temperament — are defined by the spectacle of Gregor Samsa in his bed at the outset of Franz Kafka's *The Metamorphosis* (1915), transformed into a dung beetle, and by the voice of voluptuous Molly Bloom in her bed in the last chapter of James Joyce's *Ulysses* (1922), where, during her unpunctuated, forty-five-page interior monologue, she says *yes* eighty-seven times, in a subtle orchestration of the word that rises to a famous crescendo. *Expansive* Molly, *implosive*, regressive Gregor: *Yes* versus *No*, the war in our collective psyche. *Yes/No* also provides helpful guidelines to follow in reorganizing messy book and record shelves so that when you're feeling low you can quickly find, say, a tonic Louis Armstrong or Ruby Braff or Henry "Red" Allen jazz recording — "three bugles in the sun," to paraphrase a splendid poet.

I propose that the top one or two shelves (depending on your stock) of every living-room unit of four or five bookshelves be devoted to the life-

Gaston Lachaise, *Floating Figure*, 1927 . 51¾" × 8' × 22".

affirming, celebratory works of the twentieth century. I avoid the word *modernism* here to justify shelf space for *popular culture*, which in any case is often a source for the vernacular, democratic strain in celebratory modernism. "You [should] read the prospectuses the catalogues the public notices that sing out / Here's the morning's poetry," Guillaume Apollinaire asserted in his long poem "Zone" (1913). "This morning I saw a neat street I've forgotten its name / All new and clean a bugle in the sun," he wrote, urging readers, writers, and painters alike to appreciate and appropriate "a thousand miscellaneous items" — a Whitmanesque openness that can be realized on anyone's Twentieth-Century Celebratory Shelf. This shelf (or shelves) should contain art and photography books, even of the "coffee table" variety if the images are beautiful enough; recorded music; and videocassettes of the best Astaire-Rogers movies and comic films by the likes of Laurel and Hardy, Charlie Chaplin, and Buster Keaton, which could even prove instructional. Keaton's *Sherlock Junior* (1924), for instance, offers a lucid introduction to the way self-reflexivity operates in art, motion pictures, and novels such as *Ulysses*.

Ulysses should occupy a place of honor on the top, shortest *Yes* Celebratory Shelf, flush left against the varnished wood. Nabokov, a writer whose works I happen to love, should have seven or so inches to himself there, next to Joyce. Hardcover volumes of the collected poetry of W. B. Yeats, Wallace Stevens, William Carlos Williams, Marianne Moore, and Richard Wilbur will be conspicuous for their handsome, durable spines. Ernest Hemingway could be represented by the Nick Adams stories, whose crystalline plain style and vernacular American English prose is in itself a poetic pleasure of the first order.

Choices for what ought to go on the celebratory shelf are arguable, I grant you. Serious fiction is by definition more difficult to characterize and categorize than poetry or the visual arts, and for obvious reasons. *The Waste Land* (1922) belongs on the *No* shelf, of course, next to Kafka, but William Faulkner's *The Sound and the Fury* (1929) should be on the short *Yes* shelf, close to Eudora Welty's *The Golden Apples* (1949) and Isaac Bashevis Singer's *Gimpel the Fool and Other Stories* (1957). Faulkner belongs here because his concluding Dilsey section neutralizes the furious attack of Jason Compson's preceding section. *Yes* balances *No* exquisitely, as in Alexander Calder's *Gibraltar* (frontispiece) and *Thirteen Spines* (p. 2) and Piet Mondrian's 28 ½" × 27 ¼" *Composition with Blue and Yellow* (p. 7) when they are considered in the context of their historical moment.

The sunny yellow in Mondrian's Paris composition of 1935 maintained

Piet Mondrian, *Composition with Blue and Yellow*, 1935.

its high chroma and position (11 A.M. on the solar clock) even as war clouds emanated from Nazi Germany, which had just rearmed, thereby contravening the Versailles Treaty. When Germany reoccupied the Rhineland in 1936, Calder, a Paris resident from 1926 to 1933, suspended his customary gaiety and created *Black Clouds*, an ominous mobile. Then he asserted his faith in Europe and regenerative civilization at large by imagining the universe as a badly scarred but steadfast Rock of Gibraltar (the entire work is 51 ⅞″ high). Although the "reeds" supporting *Gibraltar*'s sun and moon are similarly bent (buffeted by the proverbial winds of war), its tilted orbital plank has managed its firm gravitational hold on a spherical white conflation of mother earth and a great fish or bird egg. Has Calder's fishlike crescent moon produced this "egg"? The scale of the whale-size "moon" asks us to see an egg, while the vernacular symbolism of Gibraltar is reinforced by the Prudential Insurance Company's long use of it as their logo. *Thirteen Spines* is unambiguously regenerative. The seven-foot-high mobile was constructed in 1940, the year of total war in Europe, when Calder's materials — steel sheet, rods, wire, and aluminum, the industrial vernacular — were the essence of the German war machine on land, sea, and air. Here, in gallery space, Calder's stricken or dying black whale (Europe as Atlantis rather than Gibraltar) lies at the bottom of the sea, a one-dimensional cartoon behemoth that has nonetheless managed to project new life in the form of two biomorphic shapes — eggs or young offspring — and the thirteen lucky spines that are truly springing to the top. *Spine*, the adjective, is of course high praise in the vernacular, Calder's natural idiom. The dorsal shadow on the wall is on the beam, too, and can be read as the birth of another whale calf — *some* kind of new life, anyway — a welcome sight in 1940 as France fell and London was devastated from the air.

If one can hold the images I present in this book in the context of history, so much the better. Their excellence, however, never turns on their historical significance alone. The works belong primarily to the years between 1906 and 1945, an arbitrary but quite reasonable demarcation of the period now codified by scholars and critics as High Modernism. In 1906, Joyce wrote the story that contains the nucleus of *Ulysses*, and 1945 marks the end of World War II and includes the triumph of abstract painting: Mondrian's final, greatest works — *Broadway Boogie Woogie* (1942–43) and the unfinished *Victory Boogie Woogie* (1943–44). A reproduction of the former ought to be on your wall, next to your bed, where you could see it first thing every morning, the way a middle-class baby sees its colorful Mondrian- and Calder-derived mobile — celebratory modernism as a bright, enriching presence in one's daily life, starting at sunrise. Mondrian's *Composition with Blue and Yellow* could also be posted — the yellow square as an open window that promises an excellent day indeed. This brings me to the opening page of *Ulysses*, where Buck Mulligan, Stephen Dedalus's blasphemous roommate, stands on their balcony at 8:00 A.M. and "blessed gravely thrice the tower [where they dwell], the surrounding country and the awaking mountains." Mulligan is mocking the Catholic mass, but Joyce's image of the anthropomorphized "awaking mountains" salutes the land and elements unreservedly. "A yellow dressinggown, ungirdled, was sustained gently behind him [Mulligan] by the mild morning air," writes Joyce in the lightly alliterative second sentence of *Ulysses*, respirating the new world of the book. *Yellow* is the present book's central, symbolic color, in all its hues, from pollen and various kinds of bronze to the chroma of the sun, which shines for Molly Bloom, as her husband tells her.

Although *Ulysses* is set in Dublin and was composed in the cities of Trieste, Zurich, and Paris, it is, like Nabokov's work, informed by a love of the natural world that can be characterized loosely as pantheistic. A definition is in order. "Pantheism: the doctrine that the universe, taken or conceived of as a whole, is God; that there is no God but the combined forces and laws which are manifested in the existing universe. Pantheism is a loose designation," concludes the entry in *Webster's New International Dictionary, Second Edition.* Pantheism is a strong force in many kinds of mysticism and, like beauty, is often in the eye of the beholder, who can bring the city and country together on his or her own, risking fulsomeness in the process, as when Apollinaire addresses the Eiffel Tower as "Shepherdess [whose] flock of bridges is bleating this morning" (the second line of "Zone").

"Combined forces and laws" is a central phrase inasmuch as anthropomorphism, biomorphism, and the machine aesthetic that has been termed "mechanomorphism" are crucial to the pantheistic, celebratory sensibility. When observed from the rear, the back of Brancusi's great marble bird, *Maiastra* (1910), looks like a man in a white dress coat, an anthropomorphic or biomorphic figure at a fancy-dress ball. This fancy is the essence of the pantheistic impulse. Witness William Carlos Williams, who in his poem "The Trees" (1930) goes inside the minds of its sentient subject, out in the icy wind ("no part of us untouched"), or Alfred Stieglitz, who titled his 1922 photograph of birches *Dancing Trees* (p. 10). An adept of technology could just as easily have titled them *The Pipes.* When Anton Bruehl photographed a set of industrial gas pipes in 1927, he emphasized their resemblance to naturally twisted silver birches (p. 10, inset). Brancusi's pipe-jointed *Torso of a Young Man* executed in wood (1916) and polished bronze (1924), certainly shows its mettle (p. 11) — to pun willfully, in order to assert the fact that puns are the verbal equivalents of biomorphism, and can only help to keep us on our toes. Brancusi's bronze-limbed torso is displayed on bases of wood and limestone, implying or establishing an elemental current whose energy could be based on the (cosmic or magnetic) whirl of the wood grain. Calder's *Gibraltar* (frontispiece) is elemental, too, and pantheistic — walnut "or-

Alfred Stieglitz, *Dancing Trees*, 1922. Inset: Anton Bruehl, *Gas Works, Stamford, Connecticut*, 1927.

Opposite: Constantin Brancusi, *Torso of a Young Man*, 1924.

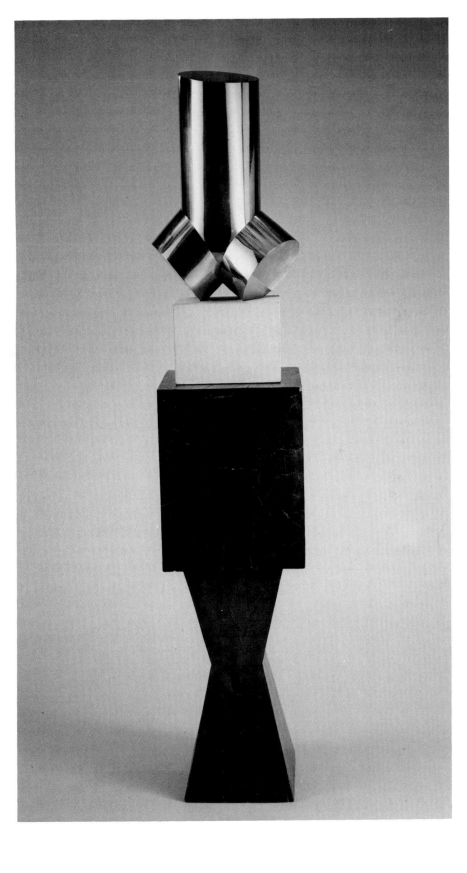

bital vapor," hard wood "rock" (lignum vitae) — its energy pipelined directly from the sun and moon, an elegant and ecologically prudent arrangement. "Trust the rock," a latter-day Apollinaire would say, compressing Prudential's motto. Then he'd try to work the phrase or the motto itself into a poem or book.

The pipe or tube, a basic form in Cubism, constitutes an excellent example of how a vernacular object or verbal expression can serve celebratory modernism in the way old-fashioned Christian iconography "worked" for Jan Van Eyck, say, in *The Arnolfino Wedding* (1434). He could assume that all his viewers would know that the little dog in the foreground of his picture represented marital fidelity. If a modern artist is intent on communicating unambiguously, what can he or she assume that *we* know? Pipes, for one thing. They are as relevant today as they ever were, and part of the lingua franca, as is Gibraltar. We refer to our own "plumbing" and, on a higher level, appraise a singer's "pipes." Pipes and tubes bring life to us in numerous ways, whether we're talking on the phone, drawing tap water, or raising the heat. If someone's success seems preordained, we say they're "pipelined." *Ulysses*, with its variety of human currents, is this book's metaphoric pipeline, and it will run through, around, and underneath the images on the following pages. And *The Arnolfino Wedding*, old as it is, will be invoked several times because its self-reflexive manner and timeless theme find expression in celebratory modernism, too.

Van Eyck and his famous painting affirm marriage, of course, as do Joyce and Gaston Lachaise, whose sculpted female figures all pay tribute to his American wife. *The Arnolfino Wedding* is a didactic statement in praise of clandestine marriages, outlawed eventually by the Council of Trent. The Arnolfinos are marrying themselves without benefit of a priest, their (profane) bedroom serving as the sacred nuptial chamber — as vast numbers must know from Art History 101 (*Esquire* magazine drew on such an assumption in their December 1988 issue, when an article on the marriage of Diane Sawyer and Mike Nichols was illustrated by a burlesqued "Arnolfino Wedding" that substituted their two faces for the ones Van Eyck painted). Van Eyck the commissioned artist honors the occasion by filling the room with recognizable religious symbols while Van Eyck the man emphasizes his affinities with these ideals by inserting himself in the room via the mirror on its back wall. *"Jan Van Eyck was here,"* he's written above the mirror in the florid cursive style of a legal document. He is one of two witnesses, both of whom are reflected in the magical mirror, along with a rear view of the newlyweds — the sort of self-reflexive gesture and device one associates with many twentieth-century writers, painters, and filmmakers. But trivial gamesmanship in all the arts has recently given self-reflexivity bad press, which makes a picture such as *The Arnolfino Wedding* even more important now as a touchstone against which to measure the seriousness of more recent self-referential works.

Van Eyck's cool statement also sets off the intensity and depth of *Ulysses*, whose affirmation of life, marriage included, is so compelling because it is asserted in the face of the kind of quiet but deadly crisis that can kill any loving relationship, all vows notwithstanding. Bluntly put (on page 736, for the first time), Mr. and Mrs. Bloom have not had "complete carnal intercourse" for "a period of 10 years, 5 months and 18 days," due to Bloom's neurotic response to the death of their infant son, Rudy, when the boy was only eleven days old (all page references are to the 1961 Modern Library edition). Prototypical modern man in the way his mind is filled with pseudoscientific data and misinformation, Mr. Bloom believes that weak semen is the cause of Rudy's death. "If it's healthy it's from the mother. If not the man. Better luck next time," he thinks, as he travels by carriage to a friend's funeral and interment in the "Hades" chapter of the novel (96).

"Next time?" One large question is implicit in *Ulysses*, though Joyce never poses it in so many words: will the Blooms, who already have a fifteen-year-old daughter (she lives elsewhere), ever cohabit again and produce another child, preferably a son? A similar question is implicit in Calder's *Gibraltar:* what sort of fish, fowl, or canned symbol could such a large egg produce, especially if it were granted a very long incubation period? The Blooms' prospects might be better if Mr. Bloom, who already carries a stony good-luck charm, had access to one of those small, portable terra cotta fertility amulets (p. 3) whose forms so appealed to Lachaise that he magnified them five thousand–fold in his veritable tribal sculpture, *Floating Figure.* "Own a piece of the rock." By modeling the lower, lateral half of her body on that of a sperm whale, Lachaise raises her to a higher power, in tandem with the Calder of *Thirteen Spines* and *Gibraltar.* Her arms are in turn raised in benediction of the land and sea, the health and natural progress of all creatures, museumgoers included: may they procreate, hatch, swim, crawl, walk, and dance.

The First Dance

Henri Matisse's monumental 8′5″ × 12′9″ painting *The Dance*, from 1910, limns a purity of mind and spirit as well as an impressive but imperfect physical grace; one woman is too humpbacked (opposite). The figures don't have genitalia, and their gender is ambiguous, though a preliminary sketch clearly depicts them as female. They are still evolving biologically. The "woman" in the center foreground seems to be swimming, and her hands recall the fingertips of God and Adam in Michelangelo's *Creation of Man* on the ceiling of the Sistine Chapel — an unfinished job here, since Matisse is sustaining and restoring a prelapsarian, asexual, tension-free world, where everything (except ritual dancing) is *luxe, calme et volupté*, the title of an earlier Matisse painting of female bathers (1904–05). The phrase is drawn from the famous refrain of Baudelaire's *L'Invitation au voyage* (1855), a poem that used to be memorized by every French schoolchild. There, in Baudelaire's utopia of the spirit, "all is order and beauty."

The poet's dream landscape is warmed and illuminated evenly by several suns, which could account for the shadow-free, saturated fields of color in *The Dance;* metaphorically, there are no shadows where there is no evil. Actually, Matisse has conflated day and night to celebrate pure, relentless color. Color doesn't serve verisimilitude. Color is consciousness. If the paint saturation or chroma isn't perfectly even, it's to remind you that a man, not God, is in charge of the vast field here. He wants to halt us in our collective, proverbial tracks and make us open our eyes, maybe for the first time. We walk before we dance.

The arrayed figures and red-ocher color suggest Greek vases of antiquity, an association that links the artist self-consciously with anonymous artisans and deathless art, the history of civilization. "I am thinking of aurochs and angels, the secret of durable pigments. . . . And this is the only immortality you and I may share, my Lolita," writes Humbert Humbert in the final sentence of *Lolita* (1955) as he wishes his book a very long life indeed. The aurochs refer to those delicate and stylized images of bison that still are visible on the cave walls of Spain and France where

Henri Matisse, *The Dance*, 1910.

they were painted ten to twenty thousand years ago — the putative temporal reach of *The Dance*, Matisse's version of the dawn of art, which may consciously allude to the *Ritual Dance* rock engraving (c. 15,000 B.C.) that is preserved in the cave of Addaura, near Palermo, Italy (see the third edition of H. W. Janson's *History of Art*, 1986, 28).

Allusiveness is characteristic of High Modernism, though references to the distant past by Matisse and Lachaise are exemplary rather than typical inasmuch as an educated viewer (a graduate of Art History 101) might well make these identifications on his or her own, without benefit of further instruction. The same cannot usually be said of the allusive treasures buried in W. B. Yeats, T. S. Eliot, James Joyce, and the later work of Nabokov. Although *auroch* isn't a household word, the above sentence from *Lolita* won't collapse if you don't know the auroch's full range. Nor does one's comprehension of the Molly Bloom section depend on special knowledge beyond a memory of the earlier events in the book. Difficulty and complexity should no longer be celebrated as artistic values per se.

The unpunctuated Molly Bloom or *Molly Bloom* (think of her section as a self-contained musical work) flows along as effortlessly as *The Dance*, as though it had been composed to a metronome. Its basic pulse, however, is faster than Matisse's, and deeply, darkly sensual where the ecstasy of the dancers is aesthetic and athletic. In *Molly Bloom*, Joyce partakes fully of his epoch's cult of the primitive and archaic, and gentler cult of the Mediterranean. Molly Bloom, who grew up on multiracial Gibraltar, embodies them all. "Id [sic] have to get a nice pair of red slippers like those Turks with the fez used to sell or yellow and a nice semitransparent morning gown," she thinks, toward the end of *Ulysses* (780), outfitting herself like one of Matisse's odalisques (harem girls) c. 1922, who were from North Africa. More specifically racial and North African is the fact that young Molly Bloom first made love by Gibraltar's "Moorish wall" (stucco and serpentine green vines by Matisse, it would seem). On the next-to-last page of *Ulysses*, Molly emphatically locates passion and abandon on the map: "The Greeks and the jews and the Arabs and the devil knows who else."

The Jungle

Aɴᴅʀᴇ́ Dᴇʀᴀɪɴ's 6′ × 7′ *The Dance*, from 1906 (below), which influenced his friend Matisse, is an early masterpiece of modernist "primitivism." Its practitioners sought to develop the innovations of Cézanne and Gauguin and the intense color attack of Van Gogh in ways that would revitalize a bloodless, moribund culture—an ambition shared by many advanced writers, composers, designers, choreographers, and dancers who would quicken everyone's pulse. They might have declared

André Derain, *The Dance*, 1906.

Janus Dog, Congo, Angola, and Zaire, Western Kongo people, c. 1900.

Wyndham Lewis, *Dancing Figures*, 1914.

together that *blood* should be the operative word and metaphor where physical performance and visceral art are concerned. Their most radical source of inspiration was the tribal art of Africa and Oceania that was then being exhibited and discussed seriously for the first time in the dim, unprepossessing ethnographic museums and galleries of Europe.

Dancing Figures, created in 1914 by Wyndham Lewis (above), demonstrates more overtly than Derain the impact of the primitive and "primitivism" on the Western artist. (Henri Rousseau's *The Dream*, of 1910 [p. 30], a touchstone of jungle civility against which to measure the others, is folk art, an aesthetically naïve work based on magazine photos and the flora and fauna that Rousseau had observed in the zoological and botanical gardens of Paris. The snake charmer is in Rousseau's picture to

Herman Leonard, *Art Blakey*, New York, 1949.

keep all beasts and dreamers in line, for now.) Although no documentation survives, Lewis's 8 ½″ × 19 ¾″ picture is probably a preliminary
study for the mural that he executed in 1915 for the Eiffel Tower restaurant in London, named for the seat of French tourism and convention-
ality, and hence the perfect locus for a call to arms, literally — a windmill
of whirling mantis arms, legs, and dynamic if not dangerous heads.

The public "primitivism" of the mural anticipates the "negritude"
vogue of the 1920s and 1930s in Europe and America, when the idea
of such a liberating force was telescoped by the title of Sherwood An-
derson's novel *Dark Laughter* (1925) and the popularity of magazine
photo-reportage such as Martin Munkácsi's 1930 shot of Congolese boys
(p. 21). On the run from bourgeois society, young Henri Cartier-Bresson

traveled to Africa in 1930 and, shortly afterwards, to Mexico and Spain, where he was able to photograph prostitutes who were literally darker than Parisian women and, he could imagine, analogous to Derain's dancers (p. 19).

Cartier-Bresson's perusal of red-light districts and other downtrodden areas was akin to such bourgeois pleasures of the time as "slumming" (a tour of the wild part of town) and an interest in "uninhibited" black dancing, from simple world's fair acts and lindy hoppers (p. 24) to the lavish but cartoon-"primitive" production numbers of Josephine Baker and nightclubs such as the Cotton Club in Harlem. Its elaborate "Black and Tan Fantasy" routine, blithely racist in conception, was played, recorded, and memorably transcended by Duke Ellington and his Jungle Band, as the great composer sometimes billed his Cotton Club Orchestra (available on *Early Ellington (1927–1934)*, RCA CD 6852-2-RB). The band's brass instruments produced a variety of eccentric or primitive "jungle" growls, moans, and wah-wah sounds by means of manipulated cup mutes, rubber plungers, bucket mutes, and swatches of felt stuffed into the bells of horns. Tribal art and the makers of modernist collages and three-dimensional assemblages of mixed media share this penchant for recycling and redeeming unlikely, vernacular materials.

As a composition, Lewis's veritable jungle floor show is dominated by triangular forms that obtrude from the top and bottom of the frame like jagged, crooked upper and lower incisors — a dance with teeth in it (surely true of Count Basie's show), projecting the possibility of lives that will have more bite, more passion, more (dark) laughter in them, starting now, after the performance. "How can we know the dancer from the dance?" asks Yeats in "Among School Children" (1927), defining dance as the preeminent, nondiscursive Symbolist art, where form and content are one.

The color symbolism of Derain's *Dance* is direct and unambiguous. The green snake, which stands for unfettered sexuality, is dancing in tandem with the bird, the branches, and the other forms. The sky is sun-saturated enough to energize everything, viewers included. (Yellow, you remember, is the signal color in these pages.) The curvilinear lines on the left-hand figure's dress, right-hand tree, and dancer's green waist-wrap (right) seem to register the sound waves of some jungle music. Green and yellow dots (left) transcribe its basic beat. Derain's central celebrant smiles lewdly or knowingly and engages male and female viewers alike

Martin Munkácsi, *Three Boys at Lake Tanganyika, the Congo,* 1930.

Ceremonial spoon, Dan tribe, Ivory Coast or Liberia.

John Gutmann, *Portrait of Count Basie*, 1939. Basie (left) and the High Hatters were appearing at the Golden Gate International Exposition (World's Fair), Treasure Island, San Francisco Bay.

Miguel Covarrubias, *The Lindy Hop*, 1936. The Mexican-born artist was active in
the United States during the 1920s and 1930s. His "celebrity" caricatures were a
regular, popular feature of the magazine *Vanity Fair*. Closely associated with the
Harlem Renaissance, his depiction of Negro life was deemed sympathetic.

Constantin Brancusi, *Blond Negress*, 1933, bronze, atop a four-part pedestal (see following page). This head is the third and virtually identical version of a work in marble executed in 1924 and 1928 titled *White Negress*.

with her snake eyes, inviting us in for one wicked dance, at least. The female slumped on the far left must have been up all night.

Cartier-Bresson's three prostitutes (p. 28) are less inviting (the central figure is a man), but their linked, natural gestures (choreographed by Matisse?) symbolically realize a primitivist's dream by showing that this multiracial, polymorphous group — a slice of sordid, lawless life — instinctively shares an affectionate communal tenderness that puts "civilization" to shame. Form and content are one, though the gender conundrum and conspicuous razor (threat or toilette?) delay our perception of the whole — a bifurcated vision, really, since the raised razor is correctly perceived as a nascent or symbolic threat, or a promise of unspeakable acts if they're one's pleasure. This *is* a jungle. And if it had been photographed in color, as travel exotica always is these days (imagine a red hat and a yellow wall), its graphic points would be softened or blunted. Conversely, if Derain's *Dance* were in black and white, and deprived of its vivacious hues, its content would come into sharper focus. In *The Wizard of Oz* (1939), reality is filmed in black and white while fantasy is in color.

The binary word-clusters *form/color* and *subject/content* telescope the terms of the continuing debate about the primitive and "primitivism," and the ways in which Eurocentric curators and scholars have misrepresented modernism's borrowings from tribal art by wrenching the latter from its original context, where it was central to the community as a body of religious and magical objects that covered every aspect of life. The Congolese *Janus Dog*, for instance (p. 18), made c. 1900 by villagers of the Western Kongo people (of wood, cloth, resin, animal teeth, shell, and iron nails), can be appreciated today as an extraordinary assemblage — something made of nothing *we'd* value, just *stuff*, whatever's at hand — like folk art and certain works by Paul Klee, especially his raggedy, fetishlike puppets. The dog's "fur" nails are inventive, and worthy

Constantin Brancusi, *Blond Negress*, a full view of the 1933 bronze on its pedestal of marble, limestone, and wood, carved by the artist in four sections (the entire work, sculpture included, is almost six feet high). The middle, circular carving looks like the cross section of a pipeline. To the calculated primitivist it's the pipeline that carries the energizing natural waters of Munkácsi's Lake Tanganyika directly into Brancusi's Paris studio, a primal enough place save for its civilized water faucets and their feeble emission of heavy, clouded chlorinated liquid.

Henri Cartier-Bresson, *Alicante, Spain*, 1933.

of admiration; the "slicked-back look" on each head is particularly good. Actually, the *Janus Dog* was once a fetish figure whose resident spirit received urgent requests from village petitioners in the form of one nail per wish. This excellent way to command attention has nothing to do with any artistic impulse, just as Wyndham Lewis's dance picture has little connection with its principal African source. The oval torso on the right of Lewis's image is adapted from one of the smooth, twenty-inch-high sculpted ceremonial spoons with hips and legs that symbolized a womb and torso. These spoons were borne by important wives of the Dan tribe of Liberia and the Ivory Coast during danced expressions of pride and at feasts where the spoons were used to distribute grain (p. 22). But the scalloped lines or scrapes on Lewis's "spoon" only do violence to the (symbolic) womb. In life, such literal scalloping would be abortive — male dynamism amok.

Derain, however, has respected his sources, including Gauguin's art — but not the romanticized legend of his escape to paradisal, colonial Tahiti. (Gauguin's highly colored autobiographical novel, *Noa Noa* [1897], and Conrad's *Heart of Darkness* [1899] are antipodal texts.) The faces of the gowned woman and the dancer on the right are modeled on an African mask from the Fang tribe of Gabon that was in Derain's possession, as is well known. Such masks represent ancestral female spirits and were used on many occasions, most of them benign. But the head of Derain's snake seems to be based on the carved, pigmented, wooden head of a sculpted ceremonial snake from Mali, used by the Dogen people in some sort of sexual initiation. To judge by the demeanor of the gowned woman, it was not a joyous occasion for everyone, or at least Derain didn't think so. Her head is heavy, her posture frozen; she may be in a trance (potions and ritual dances were sometimes supposed to induce such states). Nor does she look happy about the prospect of getting any closer to the viewer, a tourist on the wild side, a voyeur and implicit partner in a potentially compromising arrangement. Derain doesn't show any blood, but the tight grip on the initiate's arm has drained it of color. Her fingers are carefully articulated, an unusual touch amidst all these paws and thick mittens of pure color, suggesting the nerve endings of pain rather than pleasure, truly the center of *The Dance*, where Gauguin the Natural Man is enjoined by Conrad the mournful ironist of jungle-civilization, that single, fallen world. Cartier-Bresson's eerie 1929 photo of a literally shackled black mannequin in a French store window (p. 30) conflates these polarities: a symbolic Noble Savage, a relative of Munkácsi's Congolese boys, has been unhappily clothed and civilized; also, an African — the African body — has been colonized, though it's still doing better than white people, or whatever race or tribe is represented by knobbed heads and the kind of foreshortening Picasso was already practicing on *his* victims.

The gowned woman in *The Dance* is toeing the line of Derain's picture plane, in a bifurcated presentation of the primitive and "primitivism," which is distinctly an aesthetic matter for the artist — a matter of choice. This double view is unique among first-generation modernists, and is a considerable feat, achieved as it is by means of Fauvism's deliberately childlike or childish tacks (there is a difference). Anyone who has ever wielded a crayon knows that green is one of the two colors that wear out first, along with explosive red.

"Get in touch with your feelings," urges the color-coordinated green snake, whose cartoonish appearance is equal to such common diction and easy discourse. The snake, ever an expressive tribal figure, also wants us to ignore the bits and pieces of human hair, skin, and dried blood that are stuck to the insides of some of the aesthetically compelling ritual masks

Henri Cartier-Bresson, *Rouen*, 1929.

Henri Rousseau, *The Dream*, 1910. Original in color.

and brocaded, clay-covered skulls that are now on display in white-walled museums and figuratively strewn in the wake of one's discarded dance partners (e.g., Gauguin's abandoned wife, whose pain didn't find expression in his work). The evil-looking little green-and-blue beasty at the foot of the gowned "dancer" represents this collective hurt and the morally attractive nature of Derain's jungle bifurcation. Green is no longer so simple. If you look twice, the (recently initiated?) woman on the far left turns out to be slumped on a bed of green thorns — the seat of the primitive as opposed to "primitivism." The latter word often carries those qualifying quotation marks, a fair way to acknowledge that the aestheticized and loosely derivative "primitivism" of Western modernists is not by definition primitive. A certain kind of musical purist would call it "White Jazz" (the title, in fact, of a 1931 recording by Glen Gray's [white] Casa Loma Orchestra, who accepted the racialist's challenge, and, in a fast-paced number, fail to swing). Can an honorific *primitive* ever be applied without quotation marks to the work of a nontribal artist? Does John Gutmann's photo of black performers (p. 23) seem racist or racialist now because his avant-garde low-angle view and tight cropping emphasize their white gloves and ivory grins? This may be a dance with too many teeth in it.

"Primitivism" is hardly problematic in pure music (without words), or in musical prose, from *Molly Bloom* and jazz (Louis Armstrong, early Ellington, the riffing of Basie's first band [1936–40], Erroll Garner, Art Blakey's brand of bebop) to Bartók, Satie, and Stravinsky, who in 1969 complained that none of the recordings of *The Rite of Spring* (1913) were "shocking" enough. Stravinsky had not forgotten that the ballet's story includes a sacrificial death, but almost no one else remembers or cares about this. The ballet itself went into limbo after its short-lived Paris and London premiere runs (and one subsequent performance in 1920), and only the music has mattered since. It is absurd to cite the ballet's dramatic rite as the central root of modernism's putative destructive spirit (the thesis of Modris Eksteins in his *Rites of Spring: The Great War and the Birth of the Modern Age* [1989], where gas masks are said to mirror Cubist faces). Nijinsky's frenzied dancing to his own choreography in the original 1913 Ballets Russes production of *The Rite of Spring* did leave his feet and shoes bloody, which seems right in terms of self-expression and as an antidote to academism.

The visceral image of Nijinsky also establishes or reinforces the connection between athletic dancing and contemporary sports, in particular

the pleasures now offered by a mass-appeal spectator sport such as the high-level basketball played in the National Basketball Association (NBA). The sense of style displayed by even a second-string NBA player as he puts on his floor show can symbolize for viewers of any race, class, or gender the kind of self-generated joy and abandon that an admiring earlier generation would have readily identified as "primitivism" in a magazine photo such as Munkácsi's view of those black boys dashing toward Lake Tanganyika — an early version, obviously, of the fast break perfected some fifty-five years later by the Los Angeles Lakers. The phrase *black "boys,"* redolent of the overt racism of the recent past, does suggest that firm distinctions and discriminations must be made if "primitivism" is to have a continuing and enriching place in our lives, even if it doesn't go by the name of "primitivism" because we are acutely sensitive and self-conscious in matters pertaining to race. We want to free Cartier-Bresson's mannequin, of course, but save some of the symbolic essence of "primitivism" as plasma. "*Medic! Medic!*"

To dismiss Gutmann's photo now because his loose-limbed dancers are working within old minstrel conventions (white gloves, frozen grins) is to lose a chance to share their groove, to sit vicariously in Count Basie's (p. 23) or Art Blakey's (p. 19) seat of rhythm. Basie's band is riffing away, chorus after chorus, to support an airy saxophone solo by Lester Young and the efforts of the clattering hoofers, who are dancing their heads off — in thirties and forties argot they're *gone, outa sight* — so the photographer has cropped and framed them accordingly. You can lose yourself (your self, your puny self) in physical performance — you and your eye/*I*

Babe Ruth posing in front of segregated bleachers at a southern ball park prior to a spring training game, c. 1927. At least one exuberant fan wants the Babe's magic to rub off. He seems to be reaching for Ruth's aura, rather than person, a symbolic gesture that gives form to the timeless, unarticulated hopes and needs of every race (see Eudora Welty's great story "Powerhouse" [1941], about a compelling jazz primitive based on Fats Waller). If we cast the Bambino as a *Doppelgänger* of joy (our potential, our capacity for joy), then this photo documents a reversal of "primitivist"/racialist expectations: the solemn, proper black man in cap and bow tie (upper right), a mirror image of Ruth, stands for the respectable, inhibited self who might yet turn to (and into) the Babe — *White Negro I*, Brancusi would title his image of the ballplayer, and place him on a hand-carved African-esque pedestal. Ruth is still on a figurative tribal perch, more so than Henry Aaron, the black man who broke Ruth's home-run record but never showed any color, if you will.

travel elsewhere (Art Blakey's in a trance, or tribal mask—perspiration traces the "edge")—and return refreshed and renewed, the king or queen or naked princess of the jungle. Frenzied metaphors are apt here, to match the cacophony of dance music from six images, the crowd at Ruth's game, and the implications of Rousseau's large *Dream* (6′8 ½″ × 9′ 9 ½″), which could easily get wilder if the snake charmer changes his tune and the beasts come to life — in full color.

An ideal of escape and balance is struck by the regal bearing of the arms and stylized "tribal" neck and cranium of Covarrubias's central female lindy hopper. The rest of her is artistically less desirable, however, as is her partner, who is truly a "black buck" (notice his feet). He's danced most of his face away, surely a good thing since he's doubtless lost several caricatured Negroid features that would look even more stereotypical by current standards. (Would such standards force us to reject as "racist" any drawing or painting closely based on Gutmann's photo? A caricaturist of racialist bent would enlarge the High Hatters' lips, as in Paul Colin's famous 1925 poster for Josephine Baker's *La Revue Nègre*.) But the enduring lore of the Gas House Gang and attractiveness of Babe Ruth as Natural Man prove that race alone won't make you "primitive," or a fast runner. The cloven (black buck) feet of Covarrubias's male dancer remain more racist than "primitivist," however, and the pairing of his partner's glowing buttocks and the indoor jungle moon vulgarizes such painterly symbolism as Derain's green color coordination in *The Dance*. But Derain's symbolic snake is improved on on the far right of Covarrubias's little lithograph (16 ⅛″ × 11 ½″), where another pair of lindy hoppers — drawn too indistinctly to be racially offensive by any standards — makes this a bifurcated image, too. Their serpentine arm (they've already merged) projects the erotic bliss of dance in general and the specific, putative male right of spring (and every other season) that should conclude their evening together, according to *his* choreography, at least.

Basie, the essence of dignity, also experiences bliss, and without stepping out of character. He has risen from his piano bench, but not to lead the band, it seems. His eyes are closed, his hands are frozen — jazz ecstasy, the stage preceding Blakey's state. We can experience it too, some fifty years later as Basie's recorded music rattles the effete glassware on the other side of our room while we sit in the wicker jungle throne that we purchased at a Banana Republic boutique, and peruse the present book, with its reproductions of considerably more attractive examples of inte-

White Negro II: John Leonard (Pepper) Martin, who virtually invented the head-first slide, sails into third in a 1936 game against the Pittsburgh Pirates at Sportsman's Park, St. Louis (photo by an anonymous newspaper photographer for the St. Louis *Post-Dispatch*). Martin, known in the press as "The Wild Horse of the Osage" (a reference to his Oklahoma origins), was the leader of the Cardinals' high-spirited "Gas House Gang" of the 1930s. Pepper didn't wear undershorts of any kind beneath his uniform, enjoyed the largest tobacco chaw in the league, was the Gang's most inventive practical joker, played harmonica in its sui-generis country-and-western jazz ensemble, and ran the bases with abandon — a "White Negro," clearly. Brancusi notwithstanding, "White Negro" is also a dubious phrase these days — "offensive," some would say. But it's also true that African-American artists and performers have long employed stereotypical "primitivist" trappings that are open to criticism, from the painter Aaron Douglas in the 1920s to the Ethiopian Clowns in the 1930s (the barnstorming Negro baseball team whose players used aliases as comical as "Haile Selassie" and often performed in grass skirts) to the singers M. C. Hammer and Bobby McFerrin today. On the cover of his 1990 album *Medicine Music*, McFerrin's face and bare body are painted in the manner of ersatz "savages" in an old *Tarzan* movie or Cotton Club revue — worn negritude, alive and kicking.

grated "primitivism": Pepper Martin, the "White Negro," and Brancusi's *Blond Negress* (p. 25), a biracial hybrid "African" whose lips and pulled-back hairdo allow her convex Ivory Coast fertility spoon form to pass as a fish. If we looked at it in a museum, we'd be mirrored in its polished bronze surface, like the creator of *The Arnolfino Wedding*. Who wouldn't want to be there, in the deepest sense, aboard such an amphibian? Archetypes rather than stereotypes, the egg-ovoids of *Blond Negress* are coasting, or holding their own against a strong current, like salmon determined to spawn upstream. An earnest two-year-old child will purse his or her lips this way when he or she is straining to speak, but the words and sentences won't form or flow this elegantly — the history of the human race rather than a black or white issue.

Pepper Martin's headfirst slide has its unexpected depths too, especially when you look at it a second or third time and see it as something more than a pleasing example of a stock genre shot from the sports page (close play at any base). Here, a ballplayer and baseball (near the top of the frame) are racing each other to third. It's going to be a very close play, but the umpire is in a perfect position to call it, since he's exactly level with the base and third baseman — on the level, literally and figuratively. We're certain that the ump, Beans Reardon, will judge the play fairly because the distant right field foul pole is so preternaturally clear, and the primary elements of the picture are organized around it: ball, hand, fielder, grandstand, and sign-free outfield wall. Words are happily absent, because they might set off ironies that would compromise the ideals of pure play (see Huizinga's *Homo Ludens* [1944]) and the idea of a (preliterate) ideal place — some sort of pastoral. The spectators are out of focus, which helps convert the architecture and sky of Sportsman's Park (a fair name) into a handsomely arranged unit of rectangles. A child wielding crayons or felt–tipped colored pens could turn the basic geometry of the background into a veritable Mondrian. Brancusi's *Blond Negress* and its Lake Tanganyika pipeline come to mind too, for Pepper in action is better described as Pepper afloat, or levitating in a slipstream — attractive ideas, in any event. Everyone wants to move through space and time as smoothly as possible. Question from an alert reader: "Are Pepper Martin and the news photographer celebratory modernists?" Answer: No, you are, if you can accept Pepper's race to third as it's been presented here.

The Basic Beat

Picasso painted *The Race* in 1922 (below), the year of *Ulysses* and *The Waste Land*. It belongs to Molly Bloom rather than Eliot because it accepts the life of the senses quite naturally and reconciles the past and present good-naturedly (the monumentality of the "neoclassical" figures in this small 12 ⅞″ × 16 ¼″ image alludes to ancient Roman sculpture). Two years later it was used for the drop curtain of Diaghilev's Ballets Russes production of *The Blue Train*, named for the express between Paris and the Riviera, whose beaches, vacation sports, and Mediterranean sea

Pablo Picasso, *The Race*, 1922.

and sky are celebrated here, along with "Mediterraneanism" — that is, open sexuality, free of inhibiting gender definitions and conventional judgmentality. The massive front arm of the lead dancer-runner may be fending off sexual as well as athletic competitors. Even an Olympic victory on a perfect sunny day wouldn't warrant the ecstasy of her partner, whose eyes are closed — never a prudent way to run. Their path may not be altogether smooth, figuratively speaking, but the kinds of tension and moral ambiguity represented in Derain's bifurcated view have been outdistanced. Instinct and desire have won. The lead runner's ample body and aggressive Sapphic style may be a joke at the expense of Picasso's friend Gertrude Stein. Her massive front arm alludes to Rousseau's dreamer, who gestures demurely toward the beasts in the jungle, one of whom eyes her in return. But misogynistic caricature, a major mode in Picasso, is just around the bend. His gamboling female beach grotesques of the early 1930s, which are sometimes called lighthearted, look back in spirit to the jarring "primitivism" of his *Demoiselles D'Avignon* (1907), and the massive front arm before us is finally a tad too thick to be seen as an entirely friendly gesture on the part of the artist. It would be more appropriate in Covarrubias's oft-reprinted 1933 *Vanity Fair* cover caricature of a Babe Ruth whose enormous nostrils, with their capacity to draw extra oxygen, account for his prodigious appetite and power in every field.

The libretto of *The Blue Train* was written by Jean Cocteau, another free spirit, and its music was composed by Darius Milhaud, who in 1923, in Paris, had presented *The Creation of the World*, a jazz-based *ballet nègre* (the best recorded version is on *The Jazz Album*, conducted by Simon Rattle, EMI Records, CDC 7 47991 2). Jazz inspired many "serious" composers and painters of the twenties, though in *The Waste Land*, Eliot evokes jazz and cabaret music — with their hearty rhythms — as two more coarsening aspects of modern life. "O O O O that Shakespeherian [sic] Rag — / It's so elegant / So intelligent," writes Eliot, bemoaning the decline of song since the Elizabethan epoch by disposing of Cole Porter, Irving Berlin, and George and Ira Gershwin along with the worst of West End and Tin Pan Alley verse. (The best of such popular music as recorded by Ella Fitzgerald should be filed next to Milhaud on your Twentieth-Century Celebratory Shelf — Ella ahead of Sinatra for her acrobatic jazz scat singing, a very large woman's answer to *The Race* and *The Creation of the World* she won't enter or dance.)

Where Eliot evoked the art of the past ironically, to make the present appear worse (and argued that we should read *Ulysses* that way), Matisse, Lachaise, and Picasso, among others, did exactly the opposite, thereby enriching the twentieth century. The joyful energy in their sculpture and dance and beach paintings projects perfectly the idea and pulse of the willed "primitivism" of sophisticated modern artists. We're stirred by it, even now, standing alone before a huge, enveloping canvas in a museum when the crowd clears, or seated at home, looking at the pictures in this book and instant replays of bits of basketball on TV while Stravinsky or jazz plays on the phonograph, and we can wonder leisurely about some of the images here and contemplate the psychological appeal of jazz im- provisation. Can we at least *talk* our way out of a tight spot, dance away from trouble? How many nails did a Congolese villager have to hammer into a fetish figure such as the *Janus Dog* before any wish was answered? What was the percentage of success over the long run? Could you plead for the same thing again and again in a brief period? An appeals court? If you ran out of nails, could you just knock on wood? *Thump! Thump! Thump!* It's the sound made by the dancers' feet; an NBA player taking the ball downcourt; Molly Bloom's heartbeat as she thinks about the sea; Babe Ruth tapping home plate before he cocks his bat; Brancusi's mallet and chisel as he pounds into being one of his exalted birds in space or pseudo-African totem poles.

The Cusp

THIS IS CONSTANTIN BRANCUSI, photographed in his Paris studio by Edward Steichen in 1927 (opposite). On the far left is one of Brancusi's carved thirty- to forty-foot-high *Endless Columns* — "endless" because Brancusi wants them to reach as far as the viewer's spirit and imagination can soar, formal religion notwithstanding. Brancusi's various serrated columns and hefty wooden cusps were inspired by the wood carvings of many African peoples, including a tall, carved headdress from Mali; the cranium, after all, is everyone's launching area. Behind Brancusi is an egg, a prime emblem of life, of course, especially to Leopold Bloom, who is vexed by the question of fertility, which is not problematic here. On the pedestal to Brancusi's right is the marble he titled *Little Bird*, from 1925, an ovoid cut by a flat plane, representing the open mouth of a newborn bird or child (Brancusi's newborns all look very similar) reflexively announcing its arrival and considerable hunger.

Basic appetites are satisfied toward the end of *Ulysses*. Mr. Bloom, haunted all day by thoughts of his dead baby boy, brings home young Stephen Dedalus and prepares a cup of cocoa for the unhappy, bruised fellow, who's been locked out of his house, knocked down in a street fight, and rescued by Mr. Bloom. The older man's hospitality is a rare and noteworthy *social* as well as symbolic act inasmuch as impecunious, pub- and parish-oriented Dubliners simply did not "entertain" one another in their invariably chilly, threadbare houses. Perhaps Mr. Bloom has found a new friend or, as has been said often enough, a surrogate son, Telemachus to his Odysseus.

Brancusi has honored Mr. Bloom's timeless needs and ideals here, on the right, in the form of a monumentalized cup atop a "tribal" pedestal — the first cup, it seems, in the history of cups, the long, unchronicled story of nourishment and nurturing, kindness, companionship, and communion. Mr. Bloom's brand of cocoa is Epps's massproduct, emphasis on the *mass* and the sacraments of friendship — the cup as chalice. The *Table of Silence*, a monumental outdoor stone ensemble erected by Brancusi in 1937–38, at Tirgu-Jiv, in his native Romania, includes twelve of these

Edward Steichen, *Brancusi in His Studio, Paris,* 1927.

"cups," each about two feet high, which could also double as chairs — the seat of friendship, in a sort of Stonehenge of fraternity. Steichen, the photographer here, was in fact one of Brancusi's good friends, as was Joyce. Brancusi's cusp runneth over, as Joyce or Nabokov might have said. Friendship will be stressed in the following pages, at the risk of sentimentality, everyone's worst enemy.

Rising above Brancusi's egglike form is one of the sixteen marble and bronze birds in space Brancusi shaped over a twenty-five-year period. It's surprising that Steichen, whose symbolic effects could be quite overt, didn't pose Brancusi right in front of this *Bird in Space* so that it would seem to be leaping or surging out of his skull — nothing less than the transcendent spirit made visible, as though it were a headdress. As it is, the shadows on the *Endless Column* suggest a rippling, corkscrew motion that could literally take us through the roof if it were launched today.

There are many cusps in the image, partly because Steichen has staged it in the spirit and vertical manner of Brancusi's own work and the dramatic photos the sculptor himself took of his oeuvre-environment. The latter words are hyphenated because Brancusi's studio, a precursor of environmental art of the 1960s, was arranged by him as a primordial, "primitive" place inhabited by a tribe of one, though female friends did stay over. His Africanesque *Eve* (1921), carved in wood, is topped by a large, upside-down cup — the cranium as something other than an isolated, shame-filled chamber. Christian guilt must be side-stepped, even if the huge lips of Brancusi's Negro Eve give offense now as racial caricature.

Genesis

Brancusi's studio appears as it was in 1923, dominated by a marble *Bird in Space*, photographed by the sculptor, who made his own furniture, stove, pots, plates, utensils, and some 1,200 photographic prints of his own work. "Let there be light," he should have said as he snapped this picture (p. 45). The curtain is drawn to heighten the dramatic effect, and Brancusi's monumental cup is off its pedestal (below the bird), as though it's too early in creation or prehistory to be of any use yet. The ovoid on the far left could be Adam, about to have life breathed into his nostrils or just sound asleep, despite the light in his face.

Brancusi's ascending, carefully staged Stone Age assemblage, redolent of cave and temple, is as diagrammatic as his abstract portrait-drawing of Joyce that serves as the frontispiece of Richard Ellmann's biography of the writer: three spare vertical lines (probably standing for Stephen, Molly, and Mr. Bloom) and a spiral, the involuted turning that also traces the process of a self-reflexive novel such as *Ulysses*, where the seams show deliberately, and the artist is clearly the nexus, the wielder of the formidable pen or tool (the "club" in the foreground here) that will extract form from chaos. "O Jamesy let me up out of this," as Molly says to Joyce at one congested turn of her outpouring, as though she were one of Brancusi's ungainly stone slabs pleading to be liberated from its present state as it waits its turn to become perfect so it can take flight, too, or at least edge toward the light like a primordial creature stuck in some dark recess — one of the ageless tortoises of the Galápagos Islands, say, with its domed, three-hundred-pound, dull bronze shell, a potential symbol of the burden of time and all efforts to persevere. "Yea, they seemed the identical tortoises whereon the Hindoo plants this total sphere," states Melville in *The Encantadas* (1856). Brancusi's birds in space and perfect white marble *Flying Turtle* of 1940–45 — the duration of World War II, which Brancusi spent in occupied Paris — would outdistance time and rush toward eternity.

"*Eternity?*" repeats an astonished reader. Such words are scorned in sophisticated circles these days. "So why join in the vulgar laughter /

Why scorn a hereafter none can verify?" writes John Shade in Nabokov's *Pale Fire* (1962). John Shade imagines "the talks / With Socrates and Proust in cypress walks / The seraph with his six flamingo wings." The flamingo metaphor reminds us that Nabokov was a naturalist, or, more specifically, a lepidopterist. The seraph belongs to the highest order of angel. The bird and angel conjunction underscores the pantheism shared by Joyce and Nabokov, and the fact that *Lolita* and *Ulysses* end similarly, with paeans to the natural world.

"By now we find it indescribably embarrassing to mention *art* and *spirit* in the same sentence," states the critic Rosalind Krauss in the journal *October.* "Yes . . . ," says Molly Bloom on the next-to-last page of *Ulysses*, "that would do your heart good to see rivers and lakes and flowers all sorts of shapes and smells and colours springing up even out of the ditches primroses and violet nature it is as for them saying theres no God I wouldnt give a snap of my two fingers for all their learning why dont they go and create something I often asked him [her husband]." An ambitious young academic in the area of art history or literature would be at professional risk to call this passage beautiful unless he or she did so at home, or in the confessional booth.

View of Brancusi's Studio, featuring his *Bird in Space*. Photograph by Constantin Brancusi, 1923.

The Retreat

Piet Mondrian's studio-apartment in Paris, photographed in 1926 by his friend André Kertész as though it were a spiritual haven and work of art by Mondrian (opposite). It was, inasmuch as Mondrian the cloistered artist always arranged, repainted, and papered his modest dwellings to match the geometric equipoise and primary colors of the abstractions of his major period (post 1920), so many compositional permutations on red, yellow, blue, black, white, off-white, and gray — a much narrower, more challenging range of notes and chords than any composer ever faced, Arnold Schoenberg included. Music was vital to Mondrian, who painted his phonograph bright red, evidently the color that would best complement or blend with the collective sounds of the popular fox-trot and tango records he favored, surprisingly enough, since this place doesn't seem inducive to dance.

The French painter Jean Hélion, who knew Mondrian, recalled him in an interview not long before Hélion's death in 1987. "He was then living in Paris in something like seclusion — quite a warm person, really, but also distant. He looked terribly ascetic and seldom said anything. . . . I admired him unreservedly. I, too, was making abstractions. But he wanted to shut the world out, and I wanted to let it in." Hélion makes Mondrian sound like a character or creature in modern literature, one of those ground-zero descendants of Gregor Samsa who speaks to us from a lonely room, prison cell, or, in Samuel Beckett, from an ashcan or glass jar. Mondrian's drawn curtain and bare cupboard reinforce Hélion's characterization of him: the bed, with its hidden pillows and plain coverlet, looks as unsullied as a monk's. Mondrian was in fact a lifelong bachelor. But doesn't this monastic aura contradict Hélion by suggesting that the artist's retreat could also be a rewarding act of faith? The rectangle on the right-hand wall is a patch of solid color (red or blue cardboard) where we would have a mirror, and a pious Christian might display a picture of Jesus or the Madonna. The room's numinous lighting, less dramatic than Brancusi's, bespeaks a chapel or small Gothic cathedral (e.g., Robert Delaunay's 1909 painting, *St-Severin, No. 3* [p. 48]). In the terms of this

André Kertész, *Mondrian's Studio, Paris,* 1926.

Robert Delaunay, *St-Severin, No. 3*, 1909.

Opposite: Jacques Lipchitz, *Standing Personage*, 1916.

scheme of interior decoration, Mondrian's rear wall becomes an altar. The angel from Fra Angelico's *Annunciation* (c. 1440, in the San Marco monastery, Florence) might easily alight here, and stay awhile if the sounds of traffic are sufficiently muffled.

As it happens, Mondrian's ad hoc, homemade chapel is, like Lipchitz's Gothic-vaulted *Standing Personage* (p. 49), a generalized metaphor rather than a specific Christian symbol and statement of faith. Mondrian was a pantheistic Theosophist, not a Christian believer, and, as photographed by Kertész, the arrangement of his studio exemplifies, with Delaunay and Lipchitz, the way variations and improvisations on Christian sources can contribute to an uplifting but essentially secular spectacle. It's fitting that current prints of this Kertész photograph cannot fully recapture the "religious" glow of the first version (1926) — light absorbed by secularism, it would seem.

The Secular Church

THE MYTHOS AND ICONOGRAPHY of Christianity are so powerful and pervasive that non-Christians and Gentile agnostics alike draw on it to express and reify their deepest emotions. *Double Portrait with a Wineglass*, 7′ × 5′ (p. 53), was painted by Marc Chagall in his native Vitebsk, Russia, in 1917, after a sojourn in Paris from 1910 to 1913 that had exposed him to the influences of the Fauvists and such new friends as Guillaume Apollinaire and Robert Delaunay. The picture shows him on his wife's shoulders, celebrating the birth of their first and only child, a daughter, who is depicted as an angel flying above her father. Since Chagall's wife was strong enough to carry a winged, fully clothed little person to term, then why shouldn't the new mother carry him for a drink or two and also be able to walk on water? Childbirth *is* miraculous, under any circumstances, so the Jewish artist Chagall borrows and adapts Christian iconography for the occasion. His wife dwarfs the environment like Van Eyck's *Madonna in a Church* (c. 1425). Chagall is literally higher than the sun (far left), and about to lose his head over a baby.

The sky on the right suggests a typical church ceiling, but the green nimbus or aureole ("halo") around the angel is iconographically wrong (it should be gold or blue), and quite arbitrary, as is Delaunay's yellow in his *St-Severin* (p. 48), where natural light must pass through multicolored stained-glass windows and wouldn't illuminate the church's ambulatory so evenly. Its interior bulges and swells organically, pregnant with allusions to the miraculous, or so it seems. A comparison with the womblike cathedral interior of an Old Master's Annunciation would be excessive, however, since no Madonna or even Mrs. Chagall could walk on the prismatic sea that passes for a floor in Delaunay's yellow-saturated celebration of pure light, lofty form, and self-reflexive color. Chagall's arbitrary colors are more specifically self-referential, since the green of the water and Chagall's blouse, cut from the same cloth as the dancer's waist-cinch in Derain, symbolize fecundity and growth, as in any Fauvist Birth Announcement or Dance Invitation.

A Jewish sculptor, Jacques Lipchitz, goes much further than Delaunay by anthropomorphizing a cathedral (p. 49). The thin-bridged pug nose at the center of his 42 ½"–high *Standing Personage* (1916) evolves into two eyebrows that are truly arched, especially on the right, where the shadows define a curved vault (the soul? the mind?) "behind" the absent face or façade. If architecture can stand for character and destiny, then Lipchitz's limestone personage is a Gothic cathedral. Human kindness is characterized this way by Joyce and Nabokov, who is the century's greatest prose celebrant of painterly colors.

Although Mr. Bloom's father converted to Christianity, most everyone in Dublin still thinks of Leopold as a Jew, Bloom included. Yet Joyce, the lapsed Catholic, more than once associates him with Christ to pay respects to Mr. Bloom's generous and forgiving nature, as at the end of the "Cyclops" chapter, when a fantastic and amusing vision of a yellow-gowned Bloom as Elijah, whose ride in the Old Testament is said to foreshadow Christ's Ascension, shoots off to heaven in a chariot, at a forty-five-degree angle. Nabokov, who was not an observant Christian, apotheosizes his father more grandly at the end of the first chapter of *Speak, Memory* (1951), when he describes his being tossed up in the air by grateful local peasants (an old Russian custom):

> From my place at table I would suddenly see through one of the west windows a marvelous case of levitation. There, for an instant, the figure of my father in his wind-rippled white summer suit would be displayed, gloriously sprawling in midair, his limbs in a curiously casual attitude, his handsome, imperturbable features turned to the sky. Thrice, to the mighty heave-ho of his invisible tossers, he would fly up in this fashion, and the second time he would go higher than the first and then there he would be, on his last and loftiest flight, reclining, as if for good, against the cobalt blue of the summer noon, like one of those paradisiac personages who comfortably soar, with such a wealth of folds in their garments, on the vaulted ceiling of a church.

Marc Chagall, *Double Portrait with a Wineglass*, 1917.

Flight

CREATED, as related in Genesis, on the fifth day, the bird with its gift of flight symbolizes all human hopes for physical, emotional, psychological, and spiritual transport — for ecstasy and transcendence. One night, during my long and slow recovery from a heart attack, I dreamed that I was able to fly along the shore of Lake Michigan (I live near it), from Evanston to Chicago and back again, nonstop, swooping low over the water now and then — nothing showy, however, as in Chagall, Joyce, or *Star Wars* (1977). If the achievements of astronauts have rarely engaged the public's imagination, it's because their technology lags behind movie special effects and belies our collective dream or fantasy of unencumbered self-propulsion. "Free as a bird," we like to say.

The romance of flight is still reinforced by the image of the pioneer pilot alone in his open cockpit, combating the elements and, sometimes, actual birds, who saw these early, kitelike interlopers as natural enemies. Eugène Gilbert, for instance, had to shoot an eagle with his revolver while flying across the Pyrenees in the 1911 Paris-Madrid race. These pilots seem less heroic now, when their flights are seen out of context — the 23½ miles, say, that the French aviator Louis Blériot traversed in 1909, when he was the first person to fly across the English Channel. Only six years had passed since the Wright Brothers had gotten off the ground at Kitty Hawk, North Carolina, for an 852-foot flight that had lasted fifty-nine seconds.

Delaunay's 12′ × 7′ *The Cardiff Team*, from 1912–13 (opposite), is less quaint or dated than other celebrations of aeronautics because it builds from the ground up with the human form and three kinds of gravity-defiant activities aside from flying: the rugby game; a whirl on the great Ferris wheel that ran for years next to the Eiffel Tower; and a trip up the tower itself. Since its construction as part of the 1889 Paris Exposition, the tower has been a symbol of technological progress and urban dynamism, an important station for telegraph and radio antennae, and a lure for tourists who wish, in Roland Barthes's phrase, to experience "the bliss

Robert Delaunay, *The Cardiff Team*, 1912–13.

of altitude." The Ferris wheel is fashioned as an arc or parabola rather than a wheel in order to trace or imply all courses of flight and elevation in the picture. The arc connects the men and the Eiffel Tower with the ascending Astra biplane and the artist's name, which appears more boldly at the center of the action than Van Eyck's self-reflexive inscription in *The Arnolfino Wedding.* The optimistic poster (it's green, coordinated with the playing fields and Cubist planes) announces that Delaunay himself will attempt the New York–Paris air run — doubtless the painter's up-to-the-minute, topical response to the £10,000 prize offered in 1913 by Lord Northcliffe's London *Daily Mail* for the first transatlantic flight. Picasso had for some years been calling Braque "Wilbour," after Wilber Wright, an apt sobriquet for Picasso's close collaborator and pioneering adventurer in space (1908–14).

Not every artist was amused and exhilarated by the challenges posited by technology. "Painting is finished. Who could do better than that propeller? Could *you* make that?" Marcel Duchamp asked his friends Brancusi and Fernand Léger at the Exhibition of Aerial Locomotion in Paris, 1912. Brancusi's birds in space provide his answer: they look like self-propelled propellers. *The Cardiff Team* champions the Machine Age in subtler ways, too.

The frozen posture of the leaping athlete anticipates subsequent visual technologies and our attendant pleasures. He's leaping out of himself — leaping twice, really, as in an avant-garde photographer's print made from multiple negatives or deliberate double-exposures, or a Futurist painter's "slow-motion" stutter-movement savoring of velocity and power. Delaunay's "camera" has caught the athlete's arms on high, in a manner that would technically be possible only after 1925, when the Leica and other fast-action 35-mm cameras would make modern sports and dance photography possible, along with the cognate "decisive moment" quotidian photography of André Kertész, Martin Munkácsi, Friedrich Seidenstücker, and Henri Cartier-Bresson, many of whose early photographs are of everyday "sporting events" insufficiently covered by the press (a man hurdling a puddle; a girl flying straight up in the air, thanks to spontaneous joy and her billowing, winglike coattails — see *Henri Cartier-Bresson: The Early Work,* 1987, 101 and 93).

Delaunay's rugby player is poised in midair the way National Basketball Association players often are on TV after a successful slam-dunk, when they grab hold of the basket's rim with both hands and hang there momentarily, levitating — a still photo of themselves, a cadenza on an up-

Morgan Russell, *Cosmic Synchrony*, 1913–14.

tempo jazz improvisation by the Bird (Charlie Parker, that is), a florid metaphor in the spirit of the game. Then they let go, land, and immediately master space and time again on instant replay, where we can admire their takeoff and flight pattern in slow-motion, several times, too, if it's a double-pump or reverse-turn slam-dunk by the most spectacular player in the game, Michael ("Air") Jordan, who has lent his punning name to

Nike's gravity-defiant Air Jordan sneakers. Nike's name alludes to the winged Greek goddess of victory, of course; the best all-around basketball player of the 1980s is Bird (Larry, that is); and the finest writer on sports is named Angell (Roger). Delaunay pushes hard, too, to reify his airborne subjects.

As a composition, *The Cardiff Team* echoes the Ascension and Assumption altarpieces of Venetian painting. The Eiffel Tower, the great engineering feat and metaphor that Delaunay celebrates in some thirty other paintings, here looks more like one of the two spires of Notre-Dame — a conflation that reflects the fancy of Delaunay's close friend Apollinaire, who wrote, in "Zone" (1913), that the new century "climbs skywards, like Jesus," who "holds the world record for altitude." The yellow of the Astra biplane poster surely alludes to the golden-yellow hues that variously grace churches and the miraculous nimbuses in Old Master paintings of every school. Delaunay's large *Homage to Blériot* (1914) features a dazzling congeries of multicolored flat disks and wheels within wheels that blend the archetypal mandala of Eastern mysticism and the medieval Christian symbol of a harmonious, uncorrupted cosmos. The hero's monoplane is shown rising at the top of this picture, climbing straight up, vertically, a feat so truly miraculous that the plane is surrounded by a green nimbus. The academic term *High Modernism* can be applied more widely and literally than anyone has allowed. A second aircraft, a biplane, rises from the right to join Blériot, at a forty-five-degree angle (Bloom's angle), encased in no fewer than five substantial nimbuses of pink, orange, two shades of purple, and basic fecundity green — none of them the standard gold or blue of Christian iconography. Delaunay has sanctified flight and bravery in a fresh way and given those five colors a chance to appear holy for the first time. *Cosmic Synchromy* (1913–14), painted by Morgan Russell (p. 57), an American greatly influenced by Delaunay, records a nondenominational hallelujah chorus and an astronomer's dream of a trip to Jupiter.

To a nihilist and philosophical materialist such as Nathanael West, however, the sky was invariably cloudless and gray, "as if it had been rubbed with a soiled eraser. It held no angels, flaming crosses . . . [or] wheels within wheels. Only a newspaper struggled in the air like a kite with a broken spine," West writes in *Miss Lonelyhearts* (1933), shooting down Delaunay's air force, so to speak, plunging us in a despair and chaos as palpable as the "brown fog" of Eliot's "unreal City" in *The Waste Land*, where the living dead flow across London Bridge.

The End of the World

CRISES OF SELF and society merge in George Grosz's *Funeral of the Poet Panizza*, making it a primary, representative twentieth-century document (p. 61). Grosz painted it in Berlin in 1917–18, after his demobilization from the German infantry. The war was still on. He had been wounded once and then hospitalized a second time for "combat fatigue," in a ward that contained men who had been driven so wildly insane by battle that they had to be strapped to their beds. In this painting, these men seem to have sprung from their fetters to join the general population here, where madness prevails and patriotism is idiotic (the war medals, bottom right). The church, represented by the priest on the left, rushes to surrender. Strong drink is their principal means of escape, and a target of Grosz's own attack, making the 55 ⅛″ × 43 ¼″ *Funeral of the Poet Panizza* a latter-day version of Hogarth's cautionary *Gin Lane* (1751). There, the toppling masonry of a single chimney and upper wall telescopes a less advanced Chaos.

Alcohol is a pervasive, grotesque presence at the poet's open-ended funeral. Death himself, personified by the skeleton atop the coffin, is imbibing whiskey, and the bottle-bearing hippo-headed creature below the priest looks no better for the drink he's consumed. The building on the left, which reflects and emits Hell Fire, could be the first high-rise café or department store of strong drink. There is a sign or bottle on every floor, indicating that it's a bar or space reserved for drinking. The sign above the door, HEUTETANZ, means "Dance Today" — a dance in the Germanic tradition of *The Dance of Death*, no doubt, like Holbein's graphic cycle, where the skeletal title figure always larks in the foreground.

The universe is coming apart before our eyes, its accelerated rate of entropy registered by a visible fragmentation that includes language itself. On the right edge of the frame, three creatures up, a man in profile is crying out BRUD — a fragmented *Bruder*, or "brother" — which will go unheard because it's aimed offstage, and no one has ears anyway. The earless heads are amputees of a sort, and words have been severed at their figurative knees and elbows. The main *café* sign on the fourth floor (top left) is illuminated as a giant CA, which invokes *ca-ca*, the European nursery phrase for human excrement. The AL near the top of the right-hand building must be an abbreviated form of the German *All*, for "universe," "whole," and, of course, "all." All falls down, in an image of Dadaist anarchy that draws on the visual vocabulary of Cubo-Futurism while implicitly rejecting its adoration of Machine Age speed. Grosz's drunken buildings complete Hogarth's image and could be sets in an Expressionist play or motion picture whose "deep-focus" detail and clarity suggest infinite disorder.

Even if you've never seen this painting before, you should recognize its images from the frozen frames of newsreels and photos that show the panic in the streets of Shanghai and Madrid in 1937 during the first modern air raids; or from the coverage of "urban unrest" — Detroit in 1967, during the race riot that devastated the city ("It looks like Berlin in 1945," said the mayor), or in 1984, when the Tigers won the World Series and the fans ran wild, torching cars and stores. You should also recognize it as the apocalyptic nightmare city of the twentieth-century novel: Joyce's Dublin in *Ulysses* (the fantastic "Nighttown" section); Nathanael West's Los Angeles in *The Day of the Locust* (1939); Ralph Ellison's Harlem in *Invisible Man* (1952); everywhere in Thomas Pynchon's *Gravity's Rainbow* (1973). Grosz's hapless mob, his projection of mankind at large, tumbles down the street, as if into a great Boschian hole — in literature, the regressive, deathly dark paranoid underground world of Kafka's *The Burrow* (1923). Only the affirmative, uplifting forces represented by Matisse and Lachaise, Brancusi and Delaunay, Joyce and Nabokov, and Chagall's nuclear family could possibly stem this terrible slide. Let us pause for a telescopic, pedagogic visual aid.

George Grosz, *Funeral of the Poet Panizza*, 1917–18.

Visual Aid

S AUL S TEINBERG's untitled drawing from his book *The Labyrinth* (1960) depicts the struggle of POSITIVE THINKING against NEGATIVITY (opposite). Its sturdy, two-dimensional *no* can reasonably stand for Kafka's *The Castle* (1926, left unfinished at his death), a citadel and benchmark of twentieth-century nihilism that insists that all quests are ultimately quixotic and absurd, especially the idea of a published, "finished" book. *No*'s one-dimensional, delicate-limbed foe, named *Yes*, can be said to represent *Ulysses*, or, more specifically, Mr. Bloom, the knight-errant who challenges entrenched NEGATIVITY, even if he is operating on one proverbial wheel, a sexual oddfellow who is often off balance as he negotiates his way among Irishmen who consider him an outsider or, worse yet, an incarnation of the evil-eyed Wandering Jew. *No* is already leaning back. Is that a defensive posture, or is he an italic type?

The all-capital clichés of recent "psychobabble" are invoked here in the good-natured spirit of Steinberg and the nineteen images that follow, which concern typographical/topographical play, and the ways in which letters of the alphabet, words, signs, logos, graffiti, weathered surfaces, and various kinds of trashbound stuff may be invested with significance on many planes, starting from the ground up — literally, as in a photograph that was taken by André Kertész in 1944 in New York City during World War II (p. 64). The defenders of *No* would only note that the so-called citizenry has grossly (and Groszly) ignored the handmade sign in the window, "Paper is / Needed Now! / Bring it / in at / ANYTIME!" *Yes*'s supporters would find the irony amusing (the sign is not exactly a presidential message) and argue that the crudely lettered sign, with its childish drawing of a donor (too inept to be folk art), constitutes impressive evidence of grass-roots support for the war effort, an admirable State of the Union message after all. The photo is also quite touching in the way that it documents the pleasure a poor boy can find in ice cream and free reading material — visual aid in the form of the four-color Sunday comics. The boy sits comfortably atop a small corner (or microcosm) of urban chaos, the same compost heap that has enriched the modern collage

Saul Steinberg, untitled drawing, c. 1960.

maker while it has depressed or discomfited most everyone else. *Dick Tracy*, the most popular strip of the forties, still awaits the boy's perusal (it's the page claimed by his wretched left shoe; 1944, the year of this picture, produced Tracy's most colorful adversary, Flattop. "Wipe your glosses with what you know," says Joyce in *Finnegans Wake*, endorsing a democratic open eyedness).

The simple and splendid findings of Kertész the street photographer could have been recorded by Baudelaire's ideal nineteenth-century *flâneur* (a male Parisian stroller, possibly a writer or illustrator, who observed most everything); the Apollinaire of "Zone"; or by Mr. Bloom (Joyce invariably calls him "Mr.," out of respect), the advertising canvasser who covers the city out of necessity, and curiosity, his camera-eye always open to potential, unlikely sources of visual delight: "A procession

André Kertész, *New York City, October 12, 1944.*

of whitesmocked men marched slowly towards him along the gutter, scarlet sashes across their [sandwich] boards. Bargains. . . . He read the scarlet letters on their five tall white hats: H. E. L. Y. S. Wisdom Hely's [a stationer's]. Y lagging behind drew a chunk of bread from under his foreboard, crammed it into his mouth and munched as he walked" (154) — food for the eye, and an impetus to an artist such as Steinberg, who brings Mr. Bloom to bear on the world, or so he suggests in a drawing that depicts a fellow walking down the street carrying a stack of a dozen names of great characters from literature, from Ahab to Bloom. When Joyce's hero purchases a lowly piece of round, yellow soap at the chemist's to use at the public bathhouse, he savors its "sweet lemony wax" smell and the sight of bottled "orangeflower water" on the shelf. Out on the street, Bloom notices a bucket-bearing boy who is "smoking a chewed fagbutt [cigarette]. . . . Tell him if he smokes he won't grow. O let him!" thinks Bloom (71), whose dead infant son is always at the corner of his consciousness, particularly on this day, since he's going to a funeral right after the bath — elemental earth and water counterpointed by Joyce, plainly mixed and cultivated by Mr. Bloom.

The ragamuffins photographed by Cartier-Bresson in Andalusia in 1933 (p. 67) will surely grow, if spunk is any measure (*spunk*, we know from Molly Bloom, is also old Irish slang for "sperm"). The boy on the right blows fagbutt smoke at the camera, and his white scarf, a raffish touch, indicates that both boys have a sense of style, poverty notwithstanding. If the lad on the left hadn't been distracted by the photographer, he would have already donned the white rag he's holding. The chalked loop that dominates the wall behind them could be a blackboard-like visual aid aimed at them: How to Knot Your Cravat, a Guide for Slum Dandies. The boy who is feeling his way along a wall in Valencia (he must be blind), also in 1933 (p. 67), will get home safely and grow in every way if he too is empowered by imagination, the galaxylike configuration on the wall. Steinberg, who has doctored photos with pen and ink (see his 1954 collection, *The Passport*), could conceivably have drawn a cartoon thought-balloon around the affective weathered surface of the whitewashed wall to render it more clearly as a projection of the boy's mind. Fate should be as kind to us as it was to the photographer, who spotted and seized this serendipitous conjunction and has featured it in many of his books since then, including his definitive selection of 151 pictures, *Henri Cartier-Bresson: Photographer* (1979), a prime volume on anyone's Twentieth-Century Celebratory Shelf. These two photographs justify Cartier-Bresson's assertion that his entire photographic enterprise is expressed by Molly Bloom's concluding passage, which Steichen also used as the epigraph to his saccharine *Family of Man* exhibition (1955) at the Museum of Modern Art and its best-selling catalog, which has never been out of print.

Of course, it's easy to sentimentalize such Cartier-Bresson pictures or to stumble over basic issues. For forty years I've thought that the boy was blind. He's not. According to the photographer, the boy has just tossed a ball in the air and is poised to catch it. His hand is probably a foot or two from the wall. You might begin to worry about yourself if you thought he was touching the wall. Check where his feet should be and you'll see anew, and wonder. Do you jump to conclusions too quickly? How good is your depth perception? How well do you negotiate space, or, more narrowly, your own neighborhood? your pitch-black room at night, when you grope your way to the bathroom? Are you cowed by big question marks? A drawing in Steinberg's 1965 book, *The New World*, shows a man who is walking confidently along the street, carrying a thick, four-foot-long question mark under his arm as though it were a hollowed-out plaster sculpture by Jean Arp. His wife walks behind him bearing the question mark's bottom dot on her head, safari-style. Collected in Steinberg's many books, such visual aids can only lighten our own graphic burdens. Cartier-Bresson's two pictures are comforting, too, in the way that they grant us a larger margin for error by emulating the shallow space of Cubism, drawing us coolly into the game it had been playing against the conventions of illusionistic, one-point Renaissance perspective since around 1908, the year of Cartier-Bresson's birth — an indisputable, concrete fact.

Henri Cartier-Bresson, *Andalusia, Spain,* 1933.

Henri Cartier-Bresson, *Valencia, Spain,* 1933.

The Game versus the Frame

T HERE IS NOTHING QUIXOTIC about the way the Russian painter Ivan Puni addresses this white structure (opposite), his 1915 version of a public bathhouse, a common sight in provincial Russian cities, even today, because complete indoor plumbing remains a luxury. The Cyrillic letters read "Baths," the title of the 28 ¾″ × 35 ¼″ picture, too. (A Russian bathhouse contains one large indoor pool.) The outer wooden walls of such buildings are still whitewashed this hue, though they have never borne any signs — *everyone* in town knows the bath, and its dawn to dusk hours. Its important place in the community is registered by the scale of Puni's arbitrary lettering. The bathhouse is so central to Dublin that Joyce brings Bloom's new cake of yellow soap to life in fantastic Nighttown, where it rises in the east, like the sun, polishes the sky, and states aloud that it and Bloom make "a capital couple" (440). Stephen Dedalus, however, hasn't bathed in three months, a natural expression of estrangement that should ensure his isolation. Puni's apolitical, pre-Soviet red dawn projects what so grubby a fellow might feel like after a bath, especially if he's scrubbed too hard on the morning of his wedding or some other important event. *Baths* was literally painted as an act of celebration, says Puni's friend Herman Berninger (letter to the author, 1991), "created within a few hours in a spontaneous élan" after Puni had convinced two great artists and enemies, Kasimir Malevich and Vladimir Tatlin, to take part in an important exhibition that Puni was organizing.

The border or frame around Puni's fields of color serves two purposes: to remind us that the painter is challenging a flat surface, rather than trying to re-create illusionistic space, and to affirm or reaffirm the basic, everyday pleasures of life. We all frame what we prize, however mundane or inscrutable its appeal may seem to others, from a pressed dry flower to an old World Series ticket stub and *Daily News* headline, BUMS WIN! Collage (from *coller*, "to paste") comes very naturally. Art historians often make a distinction between *papier collé* and *collage*, but only the latter will be used here as a generic label.

Cubists such as Picasso, Georges Braque, and Juan Gris went further

Ivan Puni, *Baths*, 1915.

than Puni by painting their quotidian subjects within *trompe l'oeil* frames, complete with museum-style nameplates. Their collages and paintings draw on a range of techniques and open the frame democratically to include the machine-printed materials and ephemera of modern life, from wallpaper to shards of newspaper mastheads, headlines, articles, and ads, carefully clipped to form new verbal messages. *Le Journal* was their favorite paper, since its name could be truncated so winningly as LE JOU, from the verb *jouer*, of course, "to play," "to sport," "to gamble," "to gambol" — to joust with reality, like Saul Steinberg's *Yes* on its rickety wheel (*jeu* also means "game"). Imagine a squad of hunched military inspectors in lockstep, scrutinizing the ground through their magnifying glasses as they advance slowly through a mine field and mind field drawn by Steinberg. LE VRAIX ET LE FAUX states a real headline, reporting the event in Gris's *Still Life (The Table)*, from 1914. The efforts of many brave, deter-

mined men and women are commemorated by Steinberg's drawing of a
two-hundred-foot-high statue of a question mark topped by a knight-
errant on a horse, located at the center of a city square that looks like St.
Peter's in Rome (see his book *The New World*).

Like illusionistic games in earlier art and some of the best photos of
Cartier-Bresson, Cubism and Cubist *trompe l'oeil* posit basic questions:
Are our friends and associates two-faced? Do we have to see every angle
of a problem to get it right? Can we trust our eyes? Why do we feel such
panic when we take a walk in our suburban neighborhood in broad day-
light and, on our return, shoot past our house by two blocks while lost in
a daydream, then take a right turn on a quiet street we've never used
before, thinking it's ours, and suddenly wonder, *Where am I? Lost in my
own neighborhood? like a child?* "CA!" we say, or words to that effect.
Grosz's verbal fragments and downhill slant seem to suit us, though we
know we should try to follow the typographical directional signs in
School of Paris Cubism and its Russian offshoots, whose wonderfully
composed bits and pieces do not admit entropy.

Sometimes the JOU is almost lost in one of Braque's or Picasso's difficult, monochromatic experiments of 1911–12, but if your gaze is steady,
you can discern a painted JO or RHU (from RHUM, for "rum") in the murky,
shaky space, flickering away like a little, dark deep-sea fish. The JO also
summons *joie*, "joy," and an ALSE may be lurking nearby, waiting for its
hidden, shy v to come back into play (*valse* means "waltz"). In Braque's
brightly hued *Homage to J. S. Bach* (1911), the composer's name has been
applied with commercial stencils, as "Bach, J. S.," a depersonalizing
"modern" marking (as on a barracks bag or crate) that cannot compromise the deathless music, represented by Braque's cream and beige pigments. Of course, the Cubists had not gone to war yet, but those who
did, Braque especially, would return to paint even grander *trompe l'oeil*
frames around their quotidian subject matter. War is apt as a metaphor
for another problematic side of Cubism.

The extremes of Cubist verbal and visual play do seem at odds sometimes with the idea of an ennobling frame, especially when Picasso is
indulging his schoolboy penchant for obscene puns on a woman's private
parts or fragmenting *Le Journal* into a collaged URNAL, a toilet joke un-
worthy of anyone unless it's a satirical comment on the low state of the
press. Picasso's 20 5/16″ × 26 11/16″ *Glass and Bottle of Bass* (1914) is a case in
point (opposite). Picasso utilizes charcoal, pencil, India ink, white

Pablo Picasso, *Glass and Bottle of Bass*, 1914.

gouache, newspaper, and two kinds of printed wallpapers pasted on wood pulp board, but is the result much more than an exercise in extreme cleverness? Let's play the game and see.

The bottle at the center is doubly false, comprised of black ink on a pasted cutout that seems to have been stenciled in the same graphic style as the "real" brand (which still exists) until you notice that all the letters are slightly askew, especially the *B*. If you missed that, you should not venture beyond your block today. The two pieces of once-white newspaper (badly yellowed by time) are collaged to suggest a glass (note the shading), but its semicircular, handlelike opening is drawn much too small; any attempt to take a normal drink would beget a cascade of ale, a social disaster. Picasso would say that this response misses the point. You're supposed to *think* about this, not look for a literal handle. Who's ever heard of a newspaper cup? Or wallpaper framed like a masterpiece in a museum? Actually, it isn't framed so grandly, and Picasso challenges the viewer to find the truth, a tale of two wallpapers — one of them good, the other bad.

The frame has been made from the "bad" paper, and it is truly false, the kind of *trompe l'oeil* wallpaper once used as molding in fancy French homes. Even the woodlike borders are fake. Picasso dispatches decorators and pretentious bourgeois alike by undermining their effort to gild the environment. The frame turns out to be totally slapdash in execution. Its top horizontal is of uneven width, badly spliced at the right; the inside edge along the right is uneven; and the entire thing is hung crookedly. These infelicities set off the honest brightness of the floral wallpaper, which serves as both wall and floor, thanks to the white oval "table" that supports the glass and bottle. Spatial ambiguities are truly central. Unaffected gaiety should always be welcome. Without moralizing, Picasso has charted two ways of living a categorically decent life, the sort of tack one expects of Juan Gris the family man and homebody rather than Picasso the winking lion. Picasso's central wallpaper deserves a better frame, and gets one, briefly, on the top right edge, where the pompous mock-museum "molding" has "broken-off" and been replaced by a penciled and shaded *trompe l'oeil* repair job that is suitably unpretentious and dignified. The game and the frame are one — a serious exercise, after all.

As social satire or parody, *Glass and Bottle of Bass* is as good-natured as the thrust of Cubist *trompe l'oeil* in general. Unlike traditional *trompe l'oeil*, which could trick the eye badly, and hurt you if you literally walked into a painted false door (funhouses of the 1940s still offered these), the Cubists test us but telegraph their punches, telling us that space can be negotiated safely, in and above Paris, anyway. The example and practice of collage are reassuring, even poignant, now more than ever, implying as it does that machine-made detritus can still be controlled, that dead stuff is not necessarily our death knell, our Sargasso Sea. It's appropriate that current collage has "advanced" to the assemblages of a John Chamberlain, art comprised of brightly painted auto junkyard parts rather than yesterday's tempered newspaper.

The very title of Picasso's 1912 *Landscape with Posters*, an 18 ⅛" × 24" view of the city (opposite), asserts the artist's optimism and humor, since the only green in this fragmented "landscape" is its Pernod. Freed from its poster-moorings, the bottle of apéritif looks like a small monument to drinking — temperate social drinking, ideally, as opposed to the deathly

Pablo Picasso, *Landscape with Posters*, 1912.

imbibing remarked by Grosz, a World War I reality (the French and Italian infantry received a liberal wine ration and often went into battle drunk). The mauve of the Leon poster strikes an intimate note, while the white highlights on the buildings soften the façades and evoke the zinc or marbleized tabletops of outdoor cafés, where they serve Kub — the brand name of a popular bouillon cube that constitutes a broad pun, as has been pointed out several times, most recently by Kirk Varnedoe in *High and Low: Modern Art and Popular Culture* (1990). Varnedoe reproduces the original Leon poster, which looks like Picasso's but is framed clumsily, top and bottom, by the words CHAPEAUX and PARIS, and includes an accent over Léon's *e*, a bit of phonetic clutter which Picasso chose to omit from his "landscape." Varnedoe also reproduces several photos of ugly, poster-bedecked walls and advertising kiosks in Paris and New York, c. 1910, which demonstrate that commercial glut has a longer history

than we may have thought. From this evidence we can see how Picasso
has "edited" and policed the neighborhood as well as the Léon poster,
cleaning them up in order to beget an urban landscape that pleases him
more. Picasso, the imperial self, was on top of everything, it seems, even
when he was young and poor, though this approach to *Landscape with
Posters* depends on a knowledge of what urban walls looked like in 1913,
the year that the mayor of New York appointed a commission to study
and report on the excesses of billboard advertising in the city. But one
doesn't have to possess any special information to see that the Malevich
who created *Lady at the Advertising Column* (1914) was as tough and
strongwilled as any artist could be (opposite). The viewer does have to
perceive the implicit self-reflexive presence of the artist, our stand-in —
the man or woman who represents our desire to confront and order
chaos.

The lady in question (lower right) in Malevich's 26 ⅞" × 25 ¼" picture is a representative twentieth-century consumer — 1992 as well as
1914 — so inundated by an overload of messages that only her vulnerable
pale neck and hoop earring are in the clear. No wonder she's dressed in
black. It's her funeral. Her bemusement or confusion are telescoped by
the collaged words, letters, and verbal fragments that, in translation,
make no sense at all despite their exquisite deployment, which she can't
see and enjoy. The artist is in charge of this arrangement and the entire
rising column (and volume) of "ads" and meaningless photo-bits (the title
of a tabloid in *Ulysses*), which aren't about to get *him* down. He's turned
them into a visible castle in the air; the material encrustations and ba-
roque castles of thought that appear above the heads of deep-thinking
Saul Steinberg characters seem to spring from this single picture. Malevich's "castle" is warmed most conspicuously by two painterly overlays
on the collaged "mess," self-reflexive bursts of good cheer in the form of
a pink rectangle (his Léon) and a yellow square that is as sanguine as a
sunrise (lower left) or a poster that's been given a chance to start anew,
unencumbered by poorly designed typography and crowded, blurry lines
of information. Malevich's square-shouldered confidence and optimism
complement Picasso's, even if *Lady at the Advertising Column* isn't warmed
by the possibility of bouillon or some other artist-endorsed product.

Picasso's Kub sign anchors his "Kubist" composition and conjoins
painting with a more ordinary pleasure, the course followed by Puni, too,
who uses a uniform brown hue to unite four discrete areas in *Baths*: the
frame/border; the letters; and the stippling and sprinkling of brown paint

Kasimir Malevich, *Lady at the Advertising Column*, 1914.

on the separate white and red fields of color. This touch of gestural painting in advance of the fashion places the artist in his studio alone, and in
the communal pool, a social context that also has religious connotations
in *Ulysses*. Red, the color of the air, it seems, in Matisse's *Red Studio* (1911),
here stands for the delight and pleasure of others besides rhapsodic painters, however talented and tormented they may be.

Puni has achieved a more attractive and interesting self-reflexive equipoise than the prospect of total immersion in the Self, the spectacle af-
forded too often by Abstract Expressionism: huge, airless canvases
devoted to the solution of one problem alone, it seems, the crisis on the
field — the creation of, say, the Barnett Newman painting that looms before us on the museum wall. Imagine if the four Cyrillic letters on the
bathhouse only spelled PUNI. How puny, we have to add — and PUN / I, to
follow the spirited course and practice of School of Paris cutups.

The Breakfast

ALTHOUGH JUAN GRIS features his name in *Breakfast* (p. 79), he was not a solipsistic or self-indulgent artist. Structured as an ascending apex of planes reminiscent of *The Cardiff Team*, Gris's 1914 oil painting and collage is a triumph of form and substance — a rare Cubist *marriage*, which is the operative word in so domestic a scene. Its figurative depths make the 31 ⅞″ × 23 ½″ *Breakfast* worthy of a formal, institutional frame, which is provided in the Museum of Modern Art, where it's now on more or less permanent display — as permanent as collaged paper can be, given the way it naturally ages and declines, not unlike its mortal viewers.

The illusion of natural light in this "scene" is an artistic wonder and sweet irony, because it's based literally on the pasted *trompe l'oeil* wallpaper that coolly flattens and links two facets of space — the table and wall — at the same time that it contributes to the human warmth of the whole. Only the aquamarine edges and bit of white rectangle (upper left) are painted directly on the canvas; everything else is unmarked or worked-over collage. Gris's strips of paper could be cut from the same roll(s) that William Carlos Williams remarks in his poem "On Gay Wallpaper," written in 1928:

> *The green-blue ground*
> *is ruled with silver lines*
> *to say the sun is shining*
>
> *And on this moral sea*
> *of grass or dreams lie flowers*
> *or baskets of desires*
>
> *Heaven knows what they are*
> *between cerulean shapes*
> *laid regularly round*
>
> *Mat roses and tridentate*
> *leaves of gold*
> *threes, threes and threes*

writes Williams in the first half of the poem. The design on the wallpaper is threefold because three is the symbolic number for completeness of one kind or another, from religion and the theater down to a winning set of three cards of one denomination in poker. The wallpaper is "moral" because it is life enhancing, even if it's machine made, as is most of Gris's *Breakfast*, whose "allover" setting on the canvas is more filling than Picasso's "good" wallpaper in *Glass and Bottle of Bass*.

Unlike Picasso, whose newsprint glass exists to assert its artifice, Gris has realistically modeled his white coffee cups in gentle crayon to suggest that this is both a game and an imaginary room with real nourishment in it, to paraphrase Marianne Moore's famous definition of poetry. These two cups won't pun, or run over, though they do inspire rhymes. "This is for me!" says Juan Gris, by marking the spot with his name, a witty version of Van Eyck's personal testimony on marriage in *The Arnolfino Wedding*. The title of the newspaper *Le Journal* has been truncated by Gris to form another sort of rhyme. His *O* echoes the round rims of his two creamy white coffee cups and saucers — two steps up, if you will — and connects the headline Gris with the implied presence of his wife. Two, after all, is the signal domestic number, unless you're serving him/her breakfast in bed, as Mr. Bloom does, at the outset of his section of *Ulysses*, when he "move[s] about the kitchen softly, righting her breakfast things on the humpy tray" (55). The verb *righting* complements the idea of stable space, while *humpy* is a perfect colloquialism, communicating a tactile sense of a familiar object that's been warped or bent by a long life and anthropomorphized through constant use. Braque would later mix sand and sawdust into the pigments of his still lifes to communicate a visceral sense of elemental, domestic arrangements, which in Braque's instance included a long-lived, happy marriage to one woman. His early affinity for collage may be traced back to his training for the family business, house painting and decoration, though few critics would call his art "decorative" and intend it as a compliment.

Juan Gris, *Breakfast*, 1914.

Art and Decoration

TYPOGRAPHICAL PLAY also figures in Matisse, though one doesn't readily think of words as part of his pattern, whether or not you like his brand of figuration. The wallpapers, carpets, curtains, clothing, flower bouquets, and tablecloths in Matisse's Riviera paintings of 1917–47 are moral, in the sense of Williams's poem, though many critics have often disparaged these pictures for being mere "decoration" — a complaint predicated on the dictionary definition of the word ("garnish," "embellishment") and a hierarchy of genres that distinguishes between the major arts (painting, sculpture) and the minor, decorative arts (textiles, ceramics, wallpaper). This distinction would surprise ordinary people, who believe that you just fix your place up to look as good as you can, it's as simple as that. (See any collection of Farm Security Administration photographs [1935–43] for interior views of miserable rural shacks that have been neatly wallpapered with sheets of newspaper and magazine covers bearing happy seasonal images of Santa Claus and graduation day.)

Medical doctors, psychologists, and hospital administrators certainly don't accept the hierarchical distinction, because they know the degree to which all human beings are affected by the weather and their visual environment. "Winter depression called SAD is treated with light," stated the headline on Dr. Allan Bruckheim's regular "Family doctor" column in the Chicago *Tribune*, December 11, 1989. "Seasonal affective disorder," or SAD, reports Dr. Bruckheim, "is a severe form of depression that occurs each winter" and is often associated with sunlight deprivation. "In addition to psychotherapy and antidepressant medications," continues the doctor, "phototherapy may be used. Phototherapy uses a light box that provides high intensity light of about 2,500 lux (ordinary indoor light is 100 to 500 lux, while bright summer sunshine is 50,000 lux). The patient remains in front of this light box for one hour daily and is directed to look directly into the light for ten to fifteen seconds in each minute."

Because light boxes cost $360, hospital decorators have continued to brighten rooms and corridors as best they can, with cheerfully colored walls and reproductions of suitable pictures. Raoul Dufy's well-known *Homage to Mozart* (n.d.), with its gay, floral wallpaper, is very popular, and

Henri Matisse, *Yellow and Blue Interior*, 1946.

so are Georgia O'Keeffe's flowers. Matisse's little-known *Yellow and Blue Interior* (1946), a SAD-proofed picture if there ever was one, should be standard hospital issue (p. 81). It could have been painted to order for the Williams who wrote "Primrose" (1921), which begins:

> *Yellow, yellow, yellow, yellow!*
> *It is not a color.*
> *It is summer!*
> *It is the wind on a willow,*
> *the lap of waves, the shadow*
> *under a bush, a bird, a bluebird,*
> *three herons, a dead hawk*
> *rotting on a pole —*
> *Clear yellow!*

Williams, who was a physician, would probably assert that the tightly sealed hospital rooms in our latest facilities — heated or cooled by a central system — are made more depressing by the almost total absence of any natural sounds, winter or summer, another argument in favor of *Yellow and Blue Interior*, which emits the "sounds" of the rippling stria on the melons and the wind-tossed foliage on the windowlike blue screen.

Matisse understood the basic needs of the shut-in. From 1941 until his death in 1954, he had to spend most of each day in his bed or wheelchair because of a debilitating and painful intestinal ailment. He continued to work (p. 87), but it became impossible for him to visit his lush and inspiring Riviera garden, with its lemon trees. Because the heady fragrance of lemons fades quickly after they are picked, Matisse sends us fresh lemons with astonishing dispatch in *Yellow and Blue Interior*. If you perceive their blue space as a dual vision of table and sky (forget the green cup), then you can see that Matisse's still life simultaneously depicts the winged flight and landing of four hummingbird lemons. The plate is also the moon, outracing the lemons. You may not see it this way, but I'm trying to show how decorative forms can fill you with a sense of well-being and what it feels like to be well — up and around, exercising all your senses. That's my case for "decoration." Matisse delivers the goods.

Matisse was never apologetic or defensive about the decorative nature of his oeuvre. "The decorative for a work of art is an extremely precious thing," he stated in 1945, the year that World War II ended. "It does not

Henri Matisse, *Portrait of the Baroness Gourgaud,* 1924.

detract to say that the paintings of an artist are decorative." As early as
1910, he had exhibited *The Dance* under the rubric "decorative panel." Yet
the table in his 1924 *Portrait of the Baroness Gourgaud* (above) features the
influential magazine *Art et Decorat*[ion]. The title implicitly disparages
both decoration and Matisse, who is winking at the viewer by asserting
and centering the hierarchical distinction this way, seeming to join the

attack on himself (and possibly on Dufy, Derain, and Marquet) as money-hungry society artists and interior decorators who are producing blander works to suit the pretty homes of wealthy collectors such as Baron Napoléon Gourgaud and his wife. In this commissioned painting, the baroness is being read to by a companion (or secretary). Perhaps the baroness has just heard a review-essay from *Art et Decoration*, convincing her that they have wasted a lot of money on a recent Matisse, and now here he is again [groan], painting her portrait when she's in an awful mood. But maybe she really was a somber person, and the soothing words she's hearing now (the pages are smooth enough) will raise her pale spirits. That's why her companion is dressed in yellow, and is herself supported by art, or, more exactly, decorative art: the virtually tangible blossom on the tablecloth, which seems to rise up out of its flat pattern, ready to raise her own spirits, and elbow, even higher — design as an organic rather than decorative force, anti-SAD therapy before the invention of the light box.

The same holds for Matisse's other interior, where the yellow pigments and undulating blues rouse the seventy-seven-year-old artist's graphic spirit, starting with the sweeping, voluptuous lines of the Art Nouveau table leg. Its top-heavy arabesques define a pair of breasts and, on the left, a half-completed buttocks that sorely needs a thigh. "This is enough for me!" says the body language of Matisse's self-reflexive signature, its serpentine *S*s leaning toward the willing and complementary arabesques. The foot of the table leg contains the closed eye and little smile of a gentler descendant of Derain's green snake in *The Dance* (p. 19). Warmed by yellow and blue, Matisse's chair has metamorphosed into a man who is on his feet again and about to cross the room for some more paper or clay. The vase at the top of the picture is so pleased by the "green" behavior of Matisse's line that it's broken into a wild-haired jazz dance. As Williams says, yellow isn't only a color.

Matisse must have struggled to his feet quite often in 1946, when he created *Yellow and Blue Interior*, one of his last easel paintings, and attended to the finishing touches on his *Jazz* (1947), the large-format, limited-edition illustrated book that revitalized his art and life (*The Circus*, pp. 88–9, is the second colorplate in the book). *Jazz*'s twenty images are reproduced from colored-paper cutouts, a technique that became the ailing artist's main means of expression in the final years of his life, when he could no longer stand or sit before an easel. Working in bed with scissors, he "sculpted" cutouts that were pinned and rearranged on his wall by an assistant following his instructions. At their best, Matisse's cutouts represent the apotheosis of collage.

Jazz was composed in large part during the early years of the German Occupation, 1941–43, when Matisse was totally bedridden because of two intestinal operations. The images, he explained, "Derive from crystallizations of memories of circuses, folktales, and voyages." They are jazzlike because they are color improvisations on concrete subjects and themes rather than because they refer to any specific musical scenes or modes. Matisse's accompanying text, written in 1946 after the images were completed, is musical, too, and essentially *visual* — a series of "intervals," he called them, that run for three or four pages between pictures and lower the decibel level of the loud, intense colors without compromising their powerful collective rhythm (fifteen of the colorplates are double-page spreads, and the page of text reproduced here, p. 86, precedes *The Circus* in *Jazz*). The text is in Matisse's own large, even handwriting, making *Jazz* look like a secular version of a medieval illuminated manuscript. But it's really a sacred book, too, because Matisse's attempt to create and communicate felicity follows a religious impulse — Islam's more than that of any Christian sect.

The bliss of *Jazz* was achieved in the teeth of the enemy within and without — the German Occupation as the Gothic folktale's wolf at the door, represented in *Jazz* by the head of a sharp-fanged, red-eyed, unnaturally white wolf silhouetted in profile against a rectangle composed of green, blue, purple, and orange verticals (Matisse's house). The wolf should be brownish gray, of course, and its mutant or Arctic state can only symbolize the idea of unnatural laws and cold misrule (see "Design," Robert Frost's poem about mutant white). But the white wolf doesn't stand a chance against the brilliant colors of *Jazz*, where Matisse even manages to turn (Gestapo) black into a cheery color, as in *The Cowboy* (not illustrated here) and the 16 ½" × 25 ¾" *Circus*. Its scintillating black trapeze artiste (far right) is frolicking in tandem with a matching *R*. They are literally supported by yellow, and sustained on the left by the white thunder and lightning of applause and drum rolls. The blackness of the *R* emphasizes the ambiguity of the word's first syllable — *cri/cir* — a deliberate bit of wordplay that telescopes the way Matisse overrode his physical condition in the last decade of his life and turned a cry into a circus for the heart and eye. The handsome paperback edition of *Jazz* (1985) should be on the night table of every hospitalized person, like the Bible in hotel rooms.

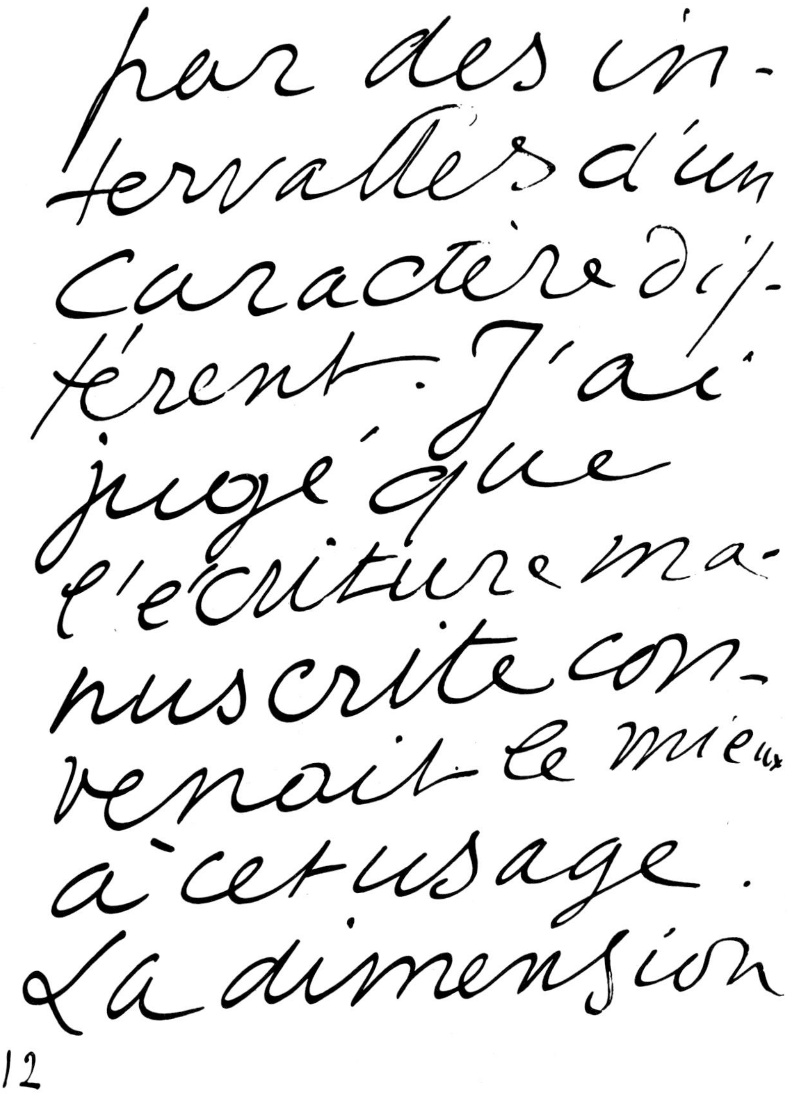

par des in-
tervalles d'un
caractère dif-
férent. J'ai
jugé que
l'écriture ma-
nuscrite con-
venait le mieux
à cet usage.
La dimension

12

Henri Matisse, page 12 of his handwritten text for *Jazz*, 1947. This is a left page facing a blank page that is followed by plate II, *The Circus*.

Matisse modeling in clay in 1951, age eighty-two. Photograph by Dmitri Kessel. Copyright © Time Warner Inc.

Overleaf: Henri Matisse, *The Circus*, in *Jazz*, 1947.

Yellow Über Alles

P AUL K LEE'S *Signs in Yellow*, 39″ × 19″ (opposite), comprises the most illegible sign system in this typographical play sequence and the "strangest" image so far in regard to medium (pastel on mounted burlap). Pronounced properly, "Clay's" name forms an apt pun in English since he and Jean Dubuffet created the most tactile pictures among twentieth-century easel painters. Earth, sand, and pebbles are mixed in with the brown and beige pigments of Dubuffet's lopsided female nudes of the 1950s to effect a flesh to filth metamorphosis akin to the alimentary landscapes of Samuel Beckett's *Molloy* (1951) — *No* traced in the mud, and worse ("Hole" and "Turdy" are towns in *Molloy*). Klee's ceaseless experimentation with surprising materials and techniques moves in the opposite direction, sometimes to testify to the possibilities of spiritual transcendence, whose path he often highlights wittily by adapting quotidian traffic signs, as in his 10 ⅝″ × 14 ¾″ watercolor on cloth, *Mural from the Temple of Longing ↖ Thither ↗*, from 1922 (p. 100). The little arrows in Klee's title constitute a visual pun of consequence since they serve ↖ *Thither* ↗ as a pair of qualifying quotation marks at the very moment that the anthropomorphized temple arch (far right, the two-legged structure beneath the largest arrow) seems to be taking a (first?) giant step in the right direction — belief in the beyond, no doubt. The shadows cast by the columns look like webbed feet — aquatic transcendence as another way over.

Although Klee's experimentation may appear solely pedagogic (he was a most responsible teacher at the Bauhaus), it is essentially pantheistic, a blending of components that quite literally affirms the elemental, by hand, in crayon, pencil, charcoal, chalk, ink, watercolor, oil, or vaporized pigments — *everything* known to adult and child — applied or sprayed on paint-primed newspaper; paper with lacquer ground; cotton on burlap; egg ground on paper; and colored paste ground mounted on card-

Paul Klee, *Signs in Yellow*, 1937.

board – to name only some of Klee's countless combinations. The pictographs and markings carved into the ground of his thickest plaster surfaces look as though they could be read by the sightless as Braille or by some archaic or primitive peoples. Klee is too studied and whimsical an artist to be called "primitive," but his elemental approach nonetheless recalls the unself-conscious work methods, materials, and spiritual mission of his colleagues in tribal cultures (the makers of the *Janus Dog*, for instance, p. 18), whose "low" materials are only natural to them, and are summoned to address the essence of life directly, which happens in Klee's late work, from the lyrical *Signs in Yellow* to *Capriccio in February*, a hard-liner (p. 97).

Boldly colored and calligraphic, the distinctive oeuvre of Klee's final years is often said to be his least accessible work. But if it's read in the context of history and Klee's own circumstances, the late work constitutes a lucid and bracing statement of comic faith. In 1933, after the National Socialists had assumed power in Germany, Klee was declared a "subversive" and "degenerate" artist and shortly afterwards was fired from his teaching position. He went into exile in Switzerland at the end of the year. In 1935, a lingering illness was diagnosed as scleroderma, an incurable disease that causes the gradual drying up of the body's fluids. (Recent medical research suggests that Klee's scleroderma was caused by long exposure to the toxic vapors of his materials.) The prolific Klee created only thirty-five new works in 1936 and then, in 1937, began to produce new art at a prodigous rate. Unlike Matisse, who lived a long life, illness notwithstanding, the fifty-six-year-old Klee was working consciously against Time, and the knowledge that many of his finest pictures were disappearing as he painted and drew. In 1937, the year that he composed *Signs in Yellow*, 102 of his pictures were confiscated by the Nazis from German museums. The famous government-sponsored "Degenerate Art" exhibition in Munich that year included seventeen of Klee's works. Like Matisse's *Yellow and Blue Interior*, Klee's yellows would generate self-healing warmth, and also thaw the icy bureaucrats of Switzerland who refused to grant Klee citizenship, even though he had been born there.

Because it returns to the color-quilt style Klee had used in the 1920s to record his firsthand impressions of North Africa, *Signs in Yellow* must be an attempt to remember and recapture a sense of those wondrous visits. But the picture is not strictly yellow, of course, which is in part a musical choice akin to Matisse's use of the text in *Jazz*. Klee would warm up for his art most mornings by playing Mozart or Bach on the violin, and the "Mozartian" tonalities of *Signs in Yellow* depend on the way Klee's peach-tinged "intervals" soften or subdue the high chromatism of yellow; unchecked, it would be too hot as music or weather — Louis Armstrong and Sidney Bechet (two of Matisse's favorites) rather than Mozart or Bach. The signs themselves influence our sense of heat and humidity by anchoring the scene in its own unique space. The quiltlike look of Klee's composition, derived from Sonia Delaunay, is a subliminal source of extra warmth or heat. Although the pastel on burlap image may look flat, its top and bottom are interchangeable "horizons," and its "sides" obey no gravity, no sense of "left" and "right," implying a multiform, four-dimensional perspective or vista (M. C. Escher comes to mind), giving form to the way intense, dry heat can envelop us, especially on the first day in such an unfamiliar climate. Klee wants to re-create the intoxicating effect of that happy, dizzying day, so many years ago, before the arrival of his literal, terrible dry season. If you had a chance to run your fingers across the surface of the picture, it might evoke hard, sun-baked earth. "Yes," says Molly Bloom on the last page of *Ulysses*. "And all the queer little streets and pink and . . . yellow houses and the rosegardens and the [yellow] jessamine and geraniums and cactuses and Gibraltar as a girl where I was a Flower of the mountain yes." A typographical touch, the capitalized *F*, aspires to accent the depth and sincerity of the simple metaphor.

Klee's black hieroglyphics, cactuses shimmering and shimmying in the artist's memory of his first view of them, clearly resemble Arabic letters and oriental ideograms, untranslatable signs — possibly from some private language that might well explain how form and color begot Nirvana for a dying artist near the end — or, more accurately, on *some* days near the end. On other days, Klee made willfully childish drawings of grotesque devils and awkward, fledgling angels. (*Childish* here means deliberately, expressively crude or inept, as opposed to *childlike*, which is stylized, charming, and *faux-naif* witty.) Klee drew these fundamental figures with a few sweeping strokes of wide-brushed black paint or colored paste applied most often to the unprimed surface of a raw newspaper page that seems to have been used only because it was on hand, the way a Surrealist writer would reach for the notepad left by the bed that night to record any rousing dreams or nightmares. Klee was working ever more quickly, as on a diary (489 new works in 1938, no fewer than 1,239 in 1939, the year before he died), though his use of newsprint shouldn't be confused with the deliberate, calm procedures of Cubist collage. Klee had no time to peruse the daily paper for clever bits and pieces. His sheets of newspaper nonetheless represent a deliberate aesthetic choice on his part, a found metaphor for the body (not the soul or self) as disposable, deteriorating matter, almost ready for the trash heap.

The torments of Klee's soul are projected rawly on newspapers in the form of anywhere from twenty to sixty squiggly black Roman letters scattered and scrambled across a field of unprimed newsprint. *What does it all mean?* they seem to ask, or rasp, from a murkier pit than the one glossed by Grosz's verbal fragments in his *Funeral of the Poet Panizza* (p. 61). Klee paints an *S* and *E* backwards, for some reason, in an uncertain, very childish hand. Even more mysterious is Klee's anti-alphabet of heavy black hyphens or dashes (raw material for arrows), slightly curved lines (aborted ideograms), thick exclamation marks (emphasizing the unsaid), and even thicker periods that appear on blank white paper as numerous neurons traveling in as many directions. "What's going on?" asks a stricken person, wide-eyed, suddenly sitting up in bed at night and addressing his or her (pain-wracked? spasmodic? ice-cold?) body as though it could or would reply — traitor that it is, showing you Death's ugly face for the first time in a hallucination that appears on your hospital wall three sleepless nights later. Jagged teeth. Pock marks. No eyes. "Late period Klee," you say to yourself, "is this It?"

Incomprehensible as they are as verbal units, Klee's agitated calligraphic markings and faltering Roman letters do spell out the kinds of organic and psychological linguistic dysfunctions that grievous illness and any concomitant stress and depression can cause: aphasia, basic dyslexia (letter reversals), stuttering, and agraphia (difficulty in writing). "Steady, steady," thinks the hospital patient, trying to write a thank-you note and, two months later, at home, straining to hold a nail in place against the wall and strike it cleanly with the hammer — one clean blow, then hang the new picture up. *Thump. Thump. Thump.* Klee's doctors must have told him that scleroderma often paralyzes the hands. Although this didn't happen to him, his "childish" graphics formulate such a possibility and confront the worst realities of linguistic dysfunction by trying out the lines, literally — a naked rehearsal, if you will. The ever-growing presence in his work of isolated, skeletal stick figures is consistent with his declining physical condition. According to his son, Felix Klee, "his esophagus had lost its elasticity. He could no longer swallow solid food — not even a grain of rice — and had to live on a liquid diet. Since he had difficulties whenever he swallowed, he always ate alone. His heart got weaker, and he had to give up . . . playing the violin. Also he lost weight, his skin tightened, and his appearance changed." Could death be far from his mind for long? *Dancing from Fear* is the title of a 1938 watercolor in which a dozen little stick figures with triangular, gray torsos hop about like animated cartoon creatures on a hot stove. Black stick figures in a 1937 Klee are truly bare boned (p. 96), and threatened by white, Death's shade in Matisse's *Jazz* and Conrad's *Heart of Darkness*, too.

Like a lover or family member, *Tod* (German for "death") often goes by its initial when it appears in the works of Klee's final years. In *Pomona Overripe* (1938), a thick circular black line suggests a head containing a face whose single beetlebrow and nose line are defined by a thick capital T. *Harbor with Sailboats* (1937), a delicately colored oil, renders boats as single horizontal lines topped by wispy linear sails or masts (lowercase *l*s). One boat, near the top of the image, is propelled by two *T*-shaped masts. A gondolalike craft in the foreground has a rudder, an oar, and a boatman in the form of a capital *P* (for *Paul*, of course). It is headed toward an imposing one-line arc — Klee's safe harbor, the shore whose field is tinted a pastel-like yellow. In *Comedians' Handbill* (1938), a thick-stemmed, white-faced "tribal dancer" is shown leaping high above the other stick figures, but no one should call him transcendent because a capital *T* is firmly established in a commanding position in the upper right-hand corner of the picture, just above an off-balance capital *K*. But in *Capriccio in February* (p. 97), painted one month later, *T* and his party get their comeuppance. You have to read the picture carefully to spot the action.

Capriccio in February is composed of oil paint on newspaper mounted on burlap, an elemental 39 ⅜″ × 29 ¼″ arrangement in which the "biodegradable" body — newsprint — has been saved and upgraded, and bad news may have been literally obliterated: any German-language Swiss newspaper of early February 1938 would have featured stories about the way Hitler had just abolished his War Ministry and taken firmer control of military planning — *T* in an even more capitol position. He would march into Vienna a few weeks later. On this February day, however, *K* is in command, taking his line for a walk (Klee's description of his procedures) as he marches around *his* town (Bern, Switzerland) in the person

Paul Klee, *The Little One Has a Day Off*, 1937.

Paul Klee, *Capriccio in February*, 1938.

of the childlike stick figure at the center of *Capriccio in February.* His
deathly white face and matching trousers identify him as Klee or his
stand-in — "walking death" is the familiar phrase — who is also identifiable by the two skinny tall *T*s that define each side of his "coat" (above
his legs) and the two black "buttons" that also serve as frightened eyes, a
state that Klee would outdistance. His stride is thus remarkably confi-
dent, like the jaunty step of the arch-leg that's bound for ↖ *Thither* ↗.
Energized by two wings of yellow, a bright red heart, and a Tyrolean hat
of hopeful green, he is raising one blue-gloved (circular) hand to greet
the top-coated stick figure on the far left. This fellow is quite unrespon-
sive, to judge by his facial expression (top left), beneath an *L*-shaped hat:
sullen, single eye line or eyebrow; sharp nose line; small, tight mouth.
Perhaps he only sees the central figure's fear-filled mouth — black rectangle, three teeth, beneath a beakish nose — and has overlooked his multiple smiles — emanations, really. He is also smiling broadly in the form
of pink-and-pale-lavender half-moons and crescents, and through the
nose, so to speak, which is at once a lopsided cartooned grin and the beak
of a pelican — a warm-weather bird drawn to the area by tropical signs of
yellow and the heat generated by the central figure's animated windmill
arms. These arms suggest four limbs in constant herky-jerky silent-film
motion, as though Buster Keaton were walking down the street doffing
his porkpie hat to everyone he passes, including a cow.

The grins and arms in question spearhead a four-pronged attack on
the enemy within and without, which includes the National Socialist
party. The "windmill arms," it turns out, also form a quixotic swastika:
graphically askew, cast adrift, looking ridiculously weak after being bodily
removed from its context, the blood-red field of the Nazi flag. *T* (upper
right corner) is doubled over, from a judo chop to the neck or a great
punch to its solar plexus. "Death, be not proud, though some have callèd
thee / Mighty and dreadful, for thou art not so," wrote John Donne in
his *Holy Sonnet X* (1633). Wallace Stevens took Death down another peg
by crowning him "The Emperor of Ice Cream" (1923), and in Faulkner's
Sanctuary (1931), a jazz band plays "I Can't Give You Anything but Love
(Baby)" at a gangster's funeral. "Poet, be seated at the piano. / Play the
present, its hoo-hoo-hoo,/ Its shoo-shoo-shoo, its ric-a-nic," writes Stevens in the first stanza of "Mozart, 1935" — the same year, it happens, that
Klee came down with scleroderma. "A Body in rags. / Be seated at the
piano," writes Stevens in the second stanza. "The snow is falling. / Strike

the piercing chord," he writes in the third stanza of "Mozart, 1935," exhorting artists to eschew sweet melody in favor of a hard-line if the times demand it. The hard-line has its rewards.

If you look again at the sullen "face," top left, and see the *L*-shaped hat as a leg, the brow as the bottom of a torso, and the nose as its second leg, then you've identified a stick figure doing the shoo-shoo-shoo or the rica-nic, dancing without fear. And if you can accept the tight mouth as the ground, then he's also hopping up and down, like a creature in an early animated cartoon film (for instance, the rat who dances the Charleston in *Alice Rattled by Rats* [1925], a forebear of Mickey Mouse. If the comparison seems frivolous or perversely pedantic, you're not in step with Klee, whose "pelican" anticipates Woody Woodpecker, b. 1940). The body language of the figure on the left is definitely in step with the Dance of Life, if not the latest shoo-shoo-shoo. The right side of his body opens up below the "shoulder," and the two resulting lines define a sleeve that can be seen as the open mouth of another creature — a penguin responding to a friendly pelican. *Capriccio in February* breaks the ice. A final series of happy metamorphoses occurs on the left as we watch the oblique line that crosses the body turn into a nose in profile, and then a chin. The hem of the fellow's coat then intersects with the newborn chin and becomes a smile. We follow this smile as it swings upward, *way* up — what a smile! — and if we let the nose and feet disappear from our field of perception, we now have a great cactus plant, attracted by signs of yellow, naturally, including the squares on a public checkerboard that in effect warns pedestrians, PERCEPTUAL GAMES IN PROGRESS / PROCEED SLOWLY / LOOK BOTH WAYS. Although the game's forms and lines overlap one another, everything seems to be played or staged on the same one-dimensional board, a characteristic of Klee's final period and scleroderma, which tightens and flattens the skin, engorging ropy sinews and forcing raised veins to implode. There is even more to decode and diagnose in *Capriccio in February*, including one or two *T*s (*T* is always around the corner), but it is clear that the figure and figurations on the left side have responded fully enough to the central fellow's warm heart and Klee's victory — his victory on this day, anyway, when, like Matisse in *Jazz*, he's managed to turn a *cri* into a little circus.

Klee reveals his heart in many of his late pictures, literally so here, in the form of the bright, stylized symbol that appears on playing cards, caricatured gently by Klee so that it stands for the truth but also mocks

Paul Klee, *Mural from the Temple of Longing ↖ Thither ↗*, 1922.

sentimental excess, the kitschy cardiovascular graphics of St. Valentine's Day and get-well cards. Any internist will tell you that the gameboards on either side of the heart serve the picture as lungs. A great anatomist and artist of illness, Klee is *Homo ludens* — man at play, in the most serious region, where "the comic and the cosmic merge" (Nabokov's phrase). As Klee wrote in his notebook around 1935, discarding the playfulness of ↖ *Thither ↗*: "We leave the here below / And build beyond instead. The land of the great Yes." It would be yellow, the color of light, God's first creation. In the foreground of *Signs in Yellow*, two "cactuses" are actually legible as *Ts — Tod* contemplated and accepted in Buddhist-like tranquility. Above and beyond them in "the sky" are two black dots — distant celestial bodies (as in Calder) or points marking the nodes of mystics and idealists such as the Russian Kasimir Malevich, whose famous Suprematist paintings, *Airplane Flying* (1915) and *White on White* (1918), are supposed to symbolize the transcendent movement(s) from one elevated state to and through another, and another again, and one more, which in Malevich's instance included the utopian Communist state. Several of the dartlike forms of his ascending "airplane" are a prescient red. His *Suprematist Painting: Eight Red Rectangles* (1915) presents an octet of levitating forms, an abstract projection of Bolshevist Ascension and Assumption that was reversed in Red Square, August 1991, when the tanks wouldn't move up and State statues tumbled over, in NBA slow motion on world TV, again and again thanks to instant replay.

Anonymous, *My Malevich*. A page from *The Post-modernism Coloring Book*, 1991. Complete by using Crayola crayon. The Crayola labeled "lemon-yellow" would be appropriate here.

Common Ground

THUMP! We're back on terra firma again, with this 1923 Soviet poster — desert yellow as propaganda (opposite). Once again the East is evoked — here, a Moslem-borne pyramid dedicated to marking the eternal worth of galoshes manufactured by Rezinotrest, the State Trust of the rubber industry. This and the second Soviet poster (p. 105) were designed by Alexander Rodchenko, the brilliant abstract painter who, after the Russian Revolution, abandoned nonfigurative art for graphic design, photography, and photomontage in order to serve the needs of the Communist party and proletariat; low literacy necessitated bold design in which to frame simple messages. Soviet critics suspended hierarchical distinctions between art and decoration. Malevich was glad to design costumes for Moscow May Day parades, Liubov Popova conceived sets for mass festivals, and no assignment or government commission was too prosaic for Rodchenko or the poet and playwright Mayakovsky, who was Rodchenko's frequent collaborator as advertising copywriter and one of the State's best boosters.

Their output in behalf of State-produced goods was prodigious, particularly after 1921, when Lenin introduced a limited free enterprise system (the NEP) to revive the faltering economy, and the government had to compete with the private sector, such as it was. Mayakovsky's advertising copy was often very clever, though the Rubbertrust is served by simple hard sell here. The galoshes, says the ad, ARE JUST A DELIGHT! / THEY'RE WORN [BY] / NORTH, WEST, SOUTH / AND / EAST. Imagine that T. S. Eliot had written ads for Lloyd's Bank in London while he served there as a clerk (1917–25) or that he'd had a hand in any of the projects of Rodchenko and Mayakovsky, from the façades they designed for State-owned department stores to caramel candy wrappers that contained a pictorial history of great victories of the Red Army where American children would find the faces of movie stars or athletes. Malevich advertised the revolution itself through his designs for the sides of the agitprop billboardlike trains that traveled across Russia in 1919 selling the Bolshevik cause to the peasants. None of his designs survive, though the agitprop

Alexander Rodchenko, advertisement for Rezinotrest galoshes, 1923.

train created for Warren Beatty's movie *Reds* (1981) gives one a splendid sense of how bold modernist colors (as in early Matisse and Puni) could serve the State by grabbing the eye of unlettered viewers.

The value of individual consciousness — an apolitical, optical matter — could still be asserted, as in the 36 ½″ × 27 ½″ Rodchenko poster that advertises the showing of six short films by Dziga Vertov (opposite). The two angled shots of the boy on the poster may valorize his group, the Pioneers (the Soviet youth corps), but he himself is gazing up at the monumentalized eye (symbol of consciousness) with such concentration that Rodchenko thinks that his effort should be filmed by Vertov's twin movie cameras. They pinpoint the edge of the wide arrowhead that compositionally recommends Vertov's six movies and a film eye that was wonderfully open to quotidian life but nonetheless always managed to promote the party line, however subtly (see Vertov's self-reflexive *Man with the Movie Camera* [1928], available on videocassette). The poster's gray tonalities evoke the silver nitrate of film stock, to affirm the new medium's vast potential for propaganda. Conformity is finally the proverbial bottom line in posters for the State.

The strict symmetry of design in each poster and the yellow-gold hues of the galoshes ad allude to the mosques of Samarkand, and their elaborate mosaics, which is apt, since Revolutionary Marxism was a nonreligious religion, a very strong secular church. The twinned figures and faces on the two posters occupy and celebrate the common ground and utopian orderliness of Communism, as opposed to the fragmentation wrought by bourgeois folly, including their recent world war (see Grosz, p. 61). Graphic design thus heralds the arrival of *The Golden Age* — the title of Shostakovich's agitprop ballet of 1930 and the saturated background color in so many Soviet posters of the time, including Rodchenko's poster for Sergei Eisenstein's film *The Battleship Potemkin* (1925), the most artistically successful propaganda export of the era.

The Rodchenko-Mayakovsky posters caused a stir at the 1925 Art Deco Exposition in Paris, especially their charming series of galoshes ads for Rezinotrest. So splendid are the galoshes in the present example that the merchants are wearing them, even in the desert, where it rarely rains. (The men are Uzbeks or Kazakhs, from Asia.) The galoshes look terribly dainty on their feet, suggesting that if Communist consumers can't afford patent-leather shoes, then this versatile footwear should satisfy every social need, formal dances included. Although the distinction of the posters

Alexander Rodchenko, *Film Eye*, 1924. A poster for six films by Dziga Vertov.
The original is almost in color — black, white, and battleship gray.

seems to rest on Rodchenko's inventive designs, they're also attractive because you feel that both he and Mayakovsky have a genuine affection for the products they are trying to sell. Mayakovsky described his ads and slogans as "street poetry," while Rodchenko lovingly called things "Comrade object," a political equivalent of the way Brancusi (p. 11) anthropomorphized and welded tubular bronze into *Torso of a Young Man*. (Malevich's c. 1925 paintings of imposing tubular peasants assert that the State's new technology will transform their lives happily and give them a bright new sheen.) But make no mistake about it: if you didn't like your Fred Astaire galoshes, there were no refunds.

In the context of history, Rodchenko's tenderness and joy are heartbreaking. His enthusiastic collaboration with Mayakovsky telescopes the ultimately tragic nature of that brief period, the 1920s, when advanced Russian artists, writers, and filmmakers served the post-Revolutionary State, or were tolerated by it, before Stalin deemed imagination an enemy in 1929 ("bourgeois formalism") and doomed artists and writers to silence or death, prison or the practice of official art, even in their own apartments: Big Brother could be watching you, with the twin cameras from Rodchenko's poster, which also look like lethal weapons, very ugly Uzis before the fact. Mayakovsky committed suicide in 1930, the same year that Rodchenko was accused of "formalism," expelled from the Association of Photographers, and abandoned by his friends. Malevich was also denounced and stripped of all authority. He reverted to a representational style of painting, a stab — it seems — at Socialist Realism that failed to restore him to favor, possibly because the Commissars of Art were intelligent enough to recognize that Malevich's version of official art wasn't altogether sincere (e.g., *The Reapers*, c. 1929–32), which today embarrasses Malevich's admirers as feckless "Socialist Realism," when in fact it goes against the grain). He died in poverty, in 1935.

The all-seeing eye (spies and informers) was everywhere. Osip Mandelstam was imprisoned for a poem known to only four other people. Rodchenko managed to live on into the 1950s, covertly painting an occasional small abstraction or realistic, sentimental portrait of a sad-faced circus clown. By this time, even the saxophone had been banned as a decadent jazz instrument, though imprisoned jazz musicians actually managed to play saxophones in clandestine jam sessions in concentration camps of the Siberian gulag. In the 1959 American foreword to *Invitation to a Beheading*, Nabokov's joyous antitotalitarian fantasy and satire of

1938, written in Hitler's Berlin, the novelist calls his book "a violin in a void." Mandelstam perished that year, in a nameless camp of the gulag. According to his widow, Nadezhda Mandelstam, in her great memoir, *Hope Against Hope* (1970), the last substantiated report of him alive depicts the poet seated in an icy prison barracks at night, encircled by a dozen or so common criminals who sat cross-legged, huddled under blankets, listening raptly as Mandelstam recited his verse from memory — a violin in the void, the possibilities of *Yes/No* seen from the darkest political perspective, on common ground.

Malevich's *The Reapers* (not illustrated), a sturdy violin, didn't feature Socialist Realism's requisite happy farmers and glowing tractors but a monumental, frontal image of a standing peasant woman (she's close to the picture plane) who holds her clenched fists by her sides and stares defiantly at the viewer and, I think, the Soviet authorities of 1932 who were then murderously punishing Malevich's native Ukraine for its refusal to collectivize its family farms (Robert Conquest's *The Harvest of Sorrow* [1986] chronicles the way Stalin engineered the "terror famine" of 1932 that killed some five million Ukrainians). Reproductions of the "rehabilitated" Malevich's monumentalized peasants (in any of his several styles) ought to be mass-produced for contemporary Russians, especially a representational work such as *The Reapers*, whose severe frontality evokes old Russian religious icons and folk art, subliminal appeals to popular taste and traditional values that make Malevich's celebration of an independent figure an even more forceful expression of present hopes for a democratic Russia or federation of democratic "ethnic" republics. The peasant woman's large, smooth, solid green skirt (almost mechano-morphic — avant-gardism on the sly, a wink from the scaffold) is set against a yellow field, *Yes* on two fronts.

The Democratic Eye,
Ear, and Nose

WHILE MANY Russian avant-gardists were producing ads and propaganda posters to reinforce the Revolution, modernists in the West such as Fernand Léger (France) and Stuart Davis (the United States) sought to celebrate quotidian life by basing entire works on commercial or vernacular sources, another kind of radical act. "Beauty is everywhere, perhaps more in your kitchen than in your eighteenth-century salon or in official museums," Léger said in 1924, the same year that Davis and Gerald Murphy respectively painted *Odol*, 24″ × 18″ (opposite) and *Razor*, 32 ⅝″ × 36 ½″ (p. 110). Davis's picture, a quite literal depiction of a bottle of Odol disinfectant, motto included, is an early product of his sustained, programmatic ambition to base his art on the American scene: "The brilliant colors on gasoline stations, chainstore fronts, and taxi-cabs . . . fast travel by trains, auto, and aeroplane, which brought new . . . perspectives; electric signs . . . 5 & 10 cent store kitchen utensils; movies and radio; Earl Hines' hot piano and Negro jazz music in general," as Davis explained in 1943. His son, Earl, was named after Hines.

Odol hardly swings at all, however. The transparent frame for which it's being fitted does distort some of the little squares pleasingly (they're from the tile floor of a bathroom or kitchen, treated to a Cubist tilt), but it's all quite inert and pretty square, to indulge the jazz idiom that Davis would often spell out, literally, in his major works. And while Odol disinfectant may have purified, it certainly couldn't have smelled too great on its own. It looks as though the product has been installed in a museum vitrine, an amusing and prescient application of Léger's remark about household beauty; the Museum of Modern Art, founded five years later, in 1929, didn't start its Design Collection until 1934. But Davis also seems to know that he hasn't gotten his act together yet and doesn't deserve a solid frame. *Odol* is noteworthy now as a piece of history, a didactic apostrophe to fellow artists, rather than a satisfactory achievement. Even by standards of commercial design the bottle alone isn't as deserving of exhibition as, say, the fountain pen in Gerald Murphy's charming *Razor*.

Although Murphy produced very few pictures (he was in business), his

Stuart Davis, *Odol*, 1924.

Gerald Murphy, *Razor*, 1924.

Razor is a signal work in the evolution of a self-conscious American vernacular art. It shows the influence of Léger, who became Murphy's close
friend (not his teacher, as some have said) during the young American's
long sojourn in France. *Razor* has been reproduced frequently, but rarely
discussed, possibly because critics are unable to see or unwilling to acknowledge that Murphy actually has a subject here: technology. The perspective is multiform, in the Cubist manner, offering at once an almost
plausible overhead view of three outsized common objects arrayed on an
assortment of furniture (desks, filing cabinets) and a head-on view of the
Safety Matches as a billboard atop a building, below which are two floating, surrealistic objects, *uncommon* in that all three were fairly recent
mass-market inventions that did indeed dominate the city to the extent
that they were improving the quality of daily life everywhere in 1924.
Better armed to face his mirror each day, the creator of *Razor* celebrates

small technological advances and the utilitarian elegance of industrial design by imitating the crossed swords or rifles of standard-issue U.S. Army
cavalry or infantry insignia, thereby producing Machine Age heraldry
(the artist had served as a noncombatant in the recent war, and men's
furnishings [as they used to be called] were his stock-in-trade in the family business, the posh Mark Cross store in New York, where the salesmen
looked like William Powell the actor). *Razor* is said to resemble an ad,
but it really doesn't, since it promotes three discrete products, a complete
incongruity—credible enough in 1992, however, which might find the
three companies owned by one Japanese conglomerate. As a pioneering
endorsement of design as art, or high applied art, *Razor* ought to be displayed prominently in the entrance gallery of the Museum of Modern
Art's Department of Architecture and Design, which is dominated by
a single-passenger 1947 Bell helicopter and bright red 1946 Italian
sports car.

William Carlos Williams, who in his poem "The Eyeglasses" (1923)
proclaimed "the universality of things," would surely be happy to have a
vintage American firetruck added to this exhibition space, one of those
vehicles whose dynamic essence he tried to capture and communicate in
"The Great Figure" (1921):

> *Among the rain*
> *and lights*
> *I saw the figure 5*
> *in gold*
> *on a red*
> *firetruck*
> *moving*
> *tense*

writes Williams in the initial lines of his thirteen-line poem. The anthropomorphizing adjective *tense* draws the reader into the scene, toward the
onrushing, clanging machine, and implies the presence of firefighters.
(The poem inspired Charles Demuth's famous posterlike painting, *I Saw
the Figure 5 in Gold* [1928], which is on display in New York's Metropolitan Museum of Art.) Is Williams's use of an almost blank page analogous
to the way a museum object, perceived in the round, is elevated, enlarged,
and clarified by the four arctic white walls and ceiling about it?

There should be no ceiling on us, according to Williams, whose firetruck poem was written on the spot, one evening in New York, after the truck had roared past him on the street. "The Red Wheelbarrow" (1923), one of Williams's shortest and most enigmatic poems, opens this way: "so much depends / upon / a red wheel / barrow." *What* depends on it? one wonders. Williams, who was a physician, would use this single red object, a striking sight next to the poem's white chickens, to measure consciousness, to take your proverbial temperature and pulse. Are you alive? Which is to say, are you alive to quotidian beauty? Its worth is glossed by the title of *My Egypt* (1927), the painting of a smokestack and two grain silos by Williams's friend Charles Demuth, who is referring to the riches of the tomb of King Tutankhamen, which had been uncovered, almost intact, in 1922, and was much discussed thereafter. Often said to be ironic, Demuth's title broadly announces that industrial and vernacular subjects are an artist's potential treasure trove — "important matters," to quote the narrator of Nabokov's little-known 1925 short story, "A Guide to Berlin" (a translated version appears in his *Details of a Sunset and Other Stories*, 1976).

"A Guide to Berlin" was written in Russian, in Berlin, when Nabokov was twenty-six, shortly after his marriage and three years after his beloved father had been assassinated there. Told in the present tense by a nameless Russian émigré, "A Guide to Berlin" opens matter-of-factly:

> In the morning I visited the Zoo and now I am entering a pub with my friend and usual pot [drinking] companion. Its sky-blue sign bears a white inscription, *Löwenbräu*, accompanied by the portrait of a lion with a winking eye and mug of beer. We sit down and I start telling my friend about utility pipes, streetcars, and other important matters.

"Other important matters" may sound ironic — a reasonable mistake, since irony is a preeminent modern tone, from Joseph Conrad through David Letterman. Moreover, Eliot's view of London as a waste land may be closer to our general sense of the contemporary city than Apollinaire's "bugle in the sun" clean street, from "Zone." Even lyrical celebrants of urban life such as André Kertész couldn't resist using commercial signs to frame ironies (opposite). But the narrator of "A Guide to Berlin" isn't being ironic. These *are* important matters, because the narrator is celebrating life, quite openly, for two reasons. First, the story was published

André Kertész, *Sécurité*, Paris, 1927.

in an émigré newspaper on December 24, 1925, and belongs to the traditional genre of the uplifting Christmas story. Second, the narrator cherishes life as a badly maimed White Army survivor of the Russian Civil War. He carries a rubber-heeled cane; his face is scarred; and, we learn on the last page, he has lost an arm. The one thousand "miscellaneous [urban] items" of Apollinaire's "Zone" look very good to him as he traverses the snow-covered, immanent city: "A young white-capped baker flashes by on his tricycle; there is something angelic about a lad dusted with flour. A van jingles past with cases on its roof containing rows of emerald-glittering empty bottles, collected from taverns. . . . But perhaps fairest of all are the carcasses, chrome yellow, with pink blotches, and arabesques, piled on a truck," and carried from it by an aproned man "across the sidewalk into the butcher's red shop" — meats by Matisse or Wallace Stevens rather than Chaim Soutine and Francis Bacon, butcher shop by Puni, who by this time was an émigré resident of Berlin.

By printing the titles of each of the story's five short sections in large, boldface type — by even having titles — Nabokov heralds the importance of these matters: THE PIPES; THE STREETCAR; WORK; EDEN (the great Berlin ZOO); THE PUB. The boldface titles are handsomely set off on the printed page, with lots of quiet, snow-white space around them. Typography confers and reinforces dignity; anthropomorphism telescopes the narrator's passionate investment in everyday life. Arrayed "In front of the house where I *live*" (emphasis added), the pipes are described as "the street's iron entrails, still idle, not yet lowered into the ground" — a condition that the narrator can appreciate. At the end of the two-page PIPES section, the *O*'s of the name *Otto*, traced in the snow at the entrance to one pipe, complement beautifully the "two orifices" of the pipes, which extend those anthropomorphized iron entrails and underscore the narrator's vision of the world as a body.

The titles alone, from THE PIPES to THE PUB, trace a happy physical and mental progression, a resurrection of a kind: from hard, icy ground — where the pipes are laid out like dead infantrymen — to warm, closed space, an inviting room where newspapers and magazines hang "like banners" to celebrate the idea of community, friendship, and security, self-renewal and new life. *The World Is Beautiful* — to use the title of the important and influential 1928 collection of formalist photographs of commonplace objects, plants, animals, machinery, and architecture that were taken by the German Albert Renger-Patzsch, another war veteran who had not been embittered by his service. The winking Löwenbräu lion — a well-designed logo in any event, still alive and in use — represents the narrator's courage, strength, resiliency, and easy good cheer. "So much depends / upon / a winking / sky-blue lion," Williams might have written. "A Guide to Berlin" is only eight pages long, but it can serve as a springboard, a quick way to gain an overview of the art of celebration, especially if you don't have time to reread *Ulysses*.

Nabokov remained alert to the poetry of the commonplace, even in *Lolita* (1955), where Humbert Humbert, who often makes mordant fun of American pop music, movies, and motels, can catch a reader by surprise by suddenly waxing lyrical: "A great user of roadside facilities, my unfastidious Lo would be charmed by toilet signs — Guys-Gals, John-Jane, Jack-Jill and even Buck's-Doe's; while lost in an artist's dream, I would stare at the honest brightness of the gasoline paraphernalia against the splendid green of oaks" — which evokes Stuart Davis's vibrant images

Walker Evans, *Shoeshine Sign in a Southern Town*, 1936.

of such paraphernalia — *Gas Pumps* (1925), for instance, where the lone utilitarian word GAS atop a pump (rather than the company's logo) underplays commerce and highlights "the honest brightness" of block lettering and abstracted vernacular form. Humbert's "artist's dream" could also be a 1950s Polaroid color snapshot by Walker Evans, whose more formal, strictly frontal black-and-white photographs of industrial paraphernalia and vernacular signs and symbols from the 1930s are still teaching us how to take delight in our unnatural, manmade environment.

In the course of documenting rural poverty for the Farm Security Administration (FSA), Evans discovered and photographed ample evidence of a bracing populist ethic and aesthetic: hand-painted and sometimes framed commercial signs and messages that express their makers' good humor and self-respect, their natural impulse toward balance, symmetry, and an uncompromising sense of elegance. The implied hero of Evans's 1936 *Shoeshine Sign in a Southern Town* (p. 115) is thus the anonymous sign-maker who wouldn't include anything so vulgar as a price list or hard-sell adjective that might dull "the honest brightness" of his SHINE. It's as though a sophisticated artist such as Puni had been able to letter BATH instinctively, without a second thought; or that Dr. Williams's compressed line and plain style were the product of tradition and habit, like a Shaker chair or utensil, rather than a hard-earned victory over Romantic and Victorian rhetoric; or that Rodchenko had omitted the twin salesmen and most of Mayakovsky's sales pitch from his galoshes ad. Less is more. "It Purifies."

The laceless state of the real white dress-shoes in Evans's picture matches the lacelessness of the painted work-shoe, limning an artist's — anyone's — utopian dream of cohesive, harmonious domains — work, home, and play — hardly a given during the Great Depression. *The People, Yes,* Carl Sandburg titled a book (1936), with more rhetorical flourish than Evans would ever allow in any of his pictures of the Depression. "His" white shoes quietly celebrate several possibilities by "dotting" the foot of each letter, turning all save *S* into exclamation points — the sort of effect subsequently favored by Saul Steinberg, who once told an interviewer that Walker Evans had "taught a generation what and how to see."

Another Evans photo, taken in South Carolina, is a classic example of his course of instruction (opposite). Note especially the FRUITS/VEGETABLES "still-life," a country cousin to Gerald Murphy's *Razor.* To be this innocent of perspective and the rules of gravity is to be truly innocent again — pure on all fronts, it would seem, an enviable state to the urbane and possibly jaded photographer who's down from the big city, accompanied by a most disheveled sidekick, James Agee (their collaborative book, *Let Us Now Praise Famous Men* [1941], came out of this trip). The local limner doesn't think of himself as innocent or untutored and has signed his painting in the lower right-hand corner, within an oval, as any serious artist would. His ability to float the produce on the picture plane like a natural-born Cubist *is* impressive, and worthy of a frame, unless they teach "Colonial Cubism" (Stuart Davis's phrase) at the art school here, which must be in the vein of 1930s progressive education, since *everything* on the porch has been awarded a frame. The photographic "collecting" and conservation of such folk images embody and celebrate a strain of native primitivism, then in its first flower in serious art circles.

Framed by Evans's camera, the shoeshine site in the first photo is as perfectly arranged as any museum display. Only the electric light might be adjusted better to illuminate the work at night, especially on Saturdays, when these shoes should be laced and out on the town, doing their stuff—like the jokey "Eye, Ear, Nose" title above this text, which, in the wake of remarks on Soviet suppression, flaunts our democratic license to make a display of ourselves.

Walker Evans, *Signs, South Carolina*, 1936.

Honest Brightness

Russell Lee's photograph of the Hi-Way Tavern, taken for the FSA in 1939, speaks to several hopes and dreams in the vernacular sign language of 1930s big business (opposite). The nameless owner of the tavern has given shape to his commercial and artistic ideas of order by arranging the foreground ads symmetrically, using the pyramid-shaped Dr. Pepper sign to top *his* approximation of a pyramid. "*My Egypt!*" Russell Lee must have thought or quipped when he stopped his car at this spot in Crystal City, Texas (1940 population 6,529). To shape his citizen-artist's dream as clearly as possible, Lee employed a long focal length on his lens, thereby squeezing together the five spatial planes before us, defined successively as we move into the picture by the Dr Pepper cluster, the large Gulf logo on the pole, the bit of truck, the Coca-Cola sign, and the stucco façade of the building. Save for the compromising shadows beneath the porch and by the pumps, the five frontal planes would appear in the photo as one flat surface, as in a Cubist painting and/or collage — School of Paris or the Colonial branch. All Quiet on the Yestern Front, and font; the typefaces don't clash. "Beauty is everywhere," as Léger said in 1924. Picasso's poster-perfect landscape seems to have come true (p. 73), Malevich in charge of putting the ads up.

The scene's wondrous balancing of no fewer than eight different products looks even better now, in the context of history, where its "honest brightness" can also stand for a satisfactory working relationship between the little guy and the System, spelling the end of the Great Depression. GOOD FOR LIFE! guarantees the tail or trailer beneath Dr. Pepper's "signature." Indeed, all but one of the products is still available. "Say 'Kraft Cheese,'" Russell Lee could well have instructed the signs, just before he snapped their picture. The idea of such a "smiling" group portrait brings to mind the equally contrived but affecting populist optimism of Frank Capra's movie *It Happened One Night* (1934), when all the strangers on a jam-packed bus, including rich girl Claudette Colbert and poor boy Clark Gable, join two scruffy vagabonds in a spirited song that becomes a community arrangement.

If Lee's scene were replicated in a realistic painting by one of Capra's

Russell Lee, *Signs in Front of a Highway Tavern, Crystal City, Texas*, 1939.

fellow travelers on this bright road — Norman Rockwell, Stevan Do-
hanos, or John Falter (cover illustrators for *The Saturday Evening Post*), or
one of the popular Regionalist artists of the day such as John Steuart
Curry, Grant Wood, Thomas Hart Benton, or Doris Lee (the photographer's first wife) — the pictures would be dismissed as propaganda in behalf of the American way. Crystal City? Grand Prize beer? "Hi-Way" as
a pun? Egregious sentimentality! But the photographic truth cannot be
gainsaid. The naïveté of the "Hi-Way" pun, repeated three times, is as
charming and welcome as the sudden, easy grin of an uncomplicated person. An abbreviated HI (left foreground) serves as a welcome mat and
seems to speak sweetly for the management like an apron-wearing host
or hostess in the doorway. In a Stuart Davis painting, such bright words
definitely speak for the artist, who, with Steinberg, Williams, and Nabokov, among others, kept his proverbial democratic eye open through the
1950s and early 1960s as the visual culture of the highway got worse and,
as the chaste superhighways appeared, was supplanted by the commercial
strip, which is the pits, man . . . like, you know, *totally!* — five low turns to
carry us into and through the vernacular 1970s and 1980s.

Brightness Hangs Tough

STEPHEN SHORE'S 1975 framing of this slice of Los Angeles is a hopeful sign (opposite). Photography aside, it represents one man's ability to stay on top of our Standard and standardized manmade environment, even if its noise and pollution sometimes make our democratic eyes, ears, and noses respectively sting, ache, and clog up. Unlike his master, Walker Evans, who would have photographed this scene at dawn, Shore hasn't tried to deny the fact of traffic or the visual clutter that could have been reduced by employing Russell Lee's Crystal City focal approach. The blur of the car on the left reminds us that this is *life*, something that art and artifice can't entirely control.

If it seems anachronistic to have produced such an image in 1975, this is in part because Pop art would seem to have exhausted a vernacular iconography that reaches back to Evans and Stuart Davis, who are often listed in academic books, essays, and museum publications as forerunners of Pop art. "With his delight in street life, commercial subject matter, and the use of lettering [Davis] anticipated many aspects of Pop Art," states the brochure that the Whitney Museum of American Art has been distributing since 1986, free of charge, to all visitors to its 20th-Century Permanent Collection. Yet "delight" isn't the root of most Pop art, especially now, as we look at it in a clearer, harder light than its first fans did thirty years ago. They welcomed Pop as democratic comic relief from the demands of hermetic, illegible Abstract Expressionism.

Although Andy Warhol may have intended his painting *200 Cans of Campbell's Tomato Soup* (1962) as little more than a latter-day Dadaist affront to Hi-Seriousness, its size and meticulously painted labels now make the 6′ × 8′ vista seem curiously literal, and depressing, as though it were the wall of an undemocratic supermarket whose manager has allowed greedy Campbell's to run wild and take over limited shelf space the way a dehumanizing consumerism and conformity are said to have overcome America during the postwar years. Perhaps the return of realism in recent years makes this picture "realistic." Certainly no one would surmise from Warhol & Co. that two-thirds of the inhabitants of the earth,

Stephen Shore, *La Brea Avenue and Beverly Boulevard, Los Angeles, California*, June 21, 1975.

who are of course wretchedly poor, would welcome an American supermarket as Paradise rather than consider it an all-encompassing symbol of
the Synthetic and Bland. Nor have art historians noted that Campbell's,
the most popular mass-produced soup (their best-seller is in fact tomato),
actually tastes good. (Does the reader recognize the radical nature of such
statements, and the courage it takes to make them?) Stuart Davis's merry
brand name depictions of manly sources of pleasure — the paintings titled
Bull Durham (1922) and *Lucky Strike* (1921), Odol in reserve to clean up
the place — have nothing whatsoever to do with Warhol's affectless irony
and parody. Even "macho" Picasso punningly saluted a favorite soup, and
Murphy's *Razor* is good-tempered steel — not irony.

In effect, Warhol's oeuvre reburies Demuth's "Egyptian" treasures.
Jasper Johns's famous twin bronzed Ballantine ale cans can serve as
mock-stately figurines on King Tut's bier — pun intended, in the spirit of
a Joycean wake for High Modernism, whose early, affectionate recycling
of everyday items (by Apollinaire, Picasso, Gris, Joyce) has also been laid
to rest by Warhol et al. Imagine the effect of a large painting of the winking Löwenbräu lion from "A Guide to Berlin." Or the impact of twenty
or forty identical little lions by Warhol. Removed from the context of the
story, the wink would take on a life of its own, variously nasty, lewd, or
smug, as if to say, "This product sucks, but who's to know, given the
cleverness of our ads and commercials." Such a Pop work would have won
the grand prize for irony, 1964. A scholar or critic could do worse than
claim 1964 as the year in which High Modernism ends or stops, with the
apotheosis of Pop art, the publication of Susan Sontag's "Notes on
Camp," and the death of Stuart Davis, the premier American democratic
modernist. Contemporary modernists such as the color photographer
Stephen Shore and the painters termed Photo-realists began resurrecting
the vernacular around 1970, to decidedly mixed reviews.

The bright vessels in the 48″ × 48″ oil painting *Blue Tile with Ice Water*
(1987), by the Photo-realist Ralph Goings (opposite), would refute Jasper
Johns's petrified ale. This adversarial pairing shouldn't be confused with
the friendly way Gris's illusionistic glassware counters Picasso's one-
dimensional version. The twist of lemon in the glass at hand gives the
liquid more weight and flavor, highlighting the relief it brings on a hot
day, especially if you come to it from the empty cans of Johns and Warhol, parched further by their brand of nihilism.

Goings's picture is a more elaborate version of the still lifes he's been

Ralph Goings, *Blue Tile with Ice Water*, 1987.

executing since around 1977 of luminous lunch-counter objects, including ketchup and mustard bottles; napkin and straw holders; sugar; crea-
mers; and salt and pepper shakers — all arranged very neatly, in various
combinations. "I've gone to so many diners, and each counter person has
his own way of arranging the objects. . . . It's a sort of personal design
statement," Goings told Linda Chase in the essay/interview that accom-
panies an illustrated survey of his career, *Ralph Goings* (1988). This might
have been said of the Hi-Way Tavern, by Russell Lee, whose tenderness

toward hard-edged subject matter has much in common with Goings, who is quite aware that his "friendly attachment" (his phrase) to his interiors is a potential trap.

In the last decade, Goings's principal subject has been the interiors of diners and restaurants. Like the other Photo-realists, he works up his paintings from photos he himself has taken. He told Linda Chase that he's omitted photographed figures from the final version of a few paintings because they were too reminiscent of Norman Rockwell, a striking admission inasmuch as several unsophisticated viewers have casually commented that Goings's diners and fast-food nooks look too good, their chrome and synthetic woods all shimmering without fail. Interested housekeepers might want the brand names of the polish and wax that can make table tiles gleam like sky-blue lake water on a bright day. Critics accuse Goings of sentimentality in the extreme, a death sentence — though it must be said that they probably never have checked out the interior of a Burger Chef restaurant, one of Ralph Goings's favorite Arcadian spots.

Such criticism, from high or low, is beside the point if you can recognize Goings's work as a contemporary, vernacular version of the timeless pastoral mode, best exemplified in America by the pantheistic nineteenth-century landscape painters who have been reclassified and revived under the name of Luminism. (A landscape is a symbolic construct, of course, as opposed to nature, which is random phenomena.) Goings's sky-blue tiles are analogous to the glowing bodies of water in the work of such Luminists as Martin Johnson Heade, Fritz Hugh Lane, and Frederick Edwin Church, where God's light sanctifies Edenic landscapes and may warm open-minded contemporary museumgoers — open-minded to the extent to which they can accept the idea of subject- and value-oriented works of art. If Goings's crystalline interiors, perused in an art gallery or book, can be accepted as idyllic, symbolic structures (forget the way a real Burger Chef *smells*), then some viewers who enter his pictures in this spirit will emerge renewed, having achieved the promise of traditional pastoral: "Tomorrow to fresh woods, and pastures new," as Milton wrote in "Lycidas." "SHINE!" exhorts Walker Evans's one-word visual poem, another version of pastoral.

Ralph Goings's brand of Luminism is very sly, however. It self-consciously insists that its fabulous state of perfection is "real" — as real, say, as the legible writing on the menu and ketchup bottle, and the fuzzy

Stephen Shore, *Trail's End Restaurant, Kanab, Utah*, August 10, 1973.

fellow in the background, who seems to be looking our way, at Goings himself as he takes the fellow's photo, which the artist surely did in the course of gathering his preparatory snapshot-"sketches." By rendering this man out of focus here, looking as blurred as he must have been in the original photograph, Goings suggests that the scene is at once a fully realized painting and a candid snapshot, too. Maybe we really will sit at this table tomorrow. The photographic truth cannot be gainsaid.

Although Goings obviously challenges official opinion and fashion, he rarely depicts food, even from a distance, and probably for two reasons. A Photo-realist close-up of photogenic food — a cake, a pie, a hot fudge sundae — would look like a *Ladies' Home Journal* ad, as Goings's own *Cream Pie* (1979) proves, the pie compromised further by an accompanying cup of black coffee. Its Luminist surface sheen looks like a fresh oil spill — industrial sabotage performed by a Pop artist such as Claes Old-enburg. His mock-monumental 4′ × 5′ stuffed "soft sculptures" of liter-ally tough-skinned plastic or canvas hamburgers and chocolate pies may actually have made it impossible to depict tasty ordinary food unless your presentation is qualified and steeled by some degree of clever irony.

Stephen Shore's 1973 color photograph of the Trail's End Restaurant, Kanab, Utah, is appealing because it doesn't varnish the apparent truth (p. 125). The angled view and shallow space, marks of Cubism, bring us closer to the table, a gameboard as challenging and amusing as a *trompe l'oeil* Cubist collage by Picasso or Gris. At first glance we may take it as an advertising spread in behalf of a restaurant chain, though there are too many items here for it to be an effective food ad, if it's effective at all. It happens that most everything on the table is a bit off, not ready for the promotional camera: the silverware is awry or tarnished, the plates are jammed together, the cantaloupe teeters on a veritable precipice, and the glasses and condiments are not lined up. Evidently the Trail's End Res-taurant is not staffed by the design-conscious personnel remarked by Ralph Goings.

The restaurant (is it part of a chain?) does try to celebrate the frontier tradition. The Formica table surface is enriched by an imitation wood grain, and the color-coordinated brown paper doilies boast sketches of life on the trail drawn in the manner of Frederic Remington and Charles Russell, the most famous artist-reporters of the vanishing ways of the Old West. The restaurant's name echoes *The End of the Trail*, the title of the famous 1918 bronze sculpture by James Earle Fraser that shows an Indian slumped on a pony, his spear lowered in defeat. The doilies mark trail's end for their art, too, especially when the kids knock over the milk or water and start turning the wet, softened Wild West into spitballs. Shore squeezes in a chair, a favorite surface in Cubist *trompe l'oeil* collage, to call attention to another false bottom — hard vinyl rather than soft frontier leather.

Consistent with the idea of typographical play and the Cubist tradition of "writing" in pictures, the table's main plate features Klee-like hiero-glyphics around its rim. These are cattle branding marks — famous ones, probably, maybe from *The Great Ranches of the American West* (an imagi-nary trail's end coffee table picture book). If this were a satirical painting (the "book's" name would be its title), the downward flight of the lone arrow on the plate would constitute a falling or failing mark for the entire

Louis Lozowick, *Still Life*, 1929. Lithograph, 10 ¼″ × 13 ¼″. The picture looks like the first and only realistic Cubo-Futurist ad for Campbell's soup, though it's hardly "still." Lozowick's converging, rushing Machine Age perspective lines bespeak a dynamic environment rather than a single table, the food as fuel located on or along the American fast track. Eat it standing up. The initial urban fast-food nooks (White Castle, Nedick's) surely got the idea from this blueprint, the upper left-hand corner of which forms an arrow, accelerating the (implied) pace even more. Grant Wood sentimentalized this domestic dynamism in many of his 1930s landscapes. Their superficial "modern" tack and Machine Age sheen may account for the brief Wood revival, c. 1982, and explain the failure of all efforts to resurrect the Old Masterish Thomas Hart Benton (Mannerism for the Masses).

enterprise, breakfast excepted. Would the food look this delicious to us (sophisticated people) if it didn't run against the grain of the small flaws, ironies, and deceptions? They draw our contempt, arouse our amusement, and isolate the natural, honest brightness of the breakfast — Stephen Shore's version of a table by Gris or Louis Lozowick (p. 127), whose two apples crowd the picture plane (the psychic space of the viewer), catch the light like sculpture, and engage our optical sense and appetite for art as well as fruit. The chess/checkerboard pattern on Lozowick's tablecloth stands for Cubist play on land, sea, and in the New West. Maybe Shore's breakfast spread is a convincing ad after all, the end move on the board, and we've bumped our noses on a *trompe l'oeil* clear glass door. Who expects anyone to extol roadside food? If one of the minimalist writers, Raymond Carver, say, wrote of his characters, "They stopped for breakfast at a Trail's End," we'd know, without another word, that the pancakes were cold and sodden.

It's too late in the game to ask or expect good-looking, ordinary food to defy gravity, as in Lozowick, or stand alone, unprotected — the way simple, succulent plums were preserved in the 1920s in paintings by Charles Demuth and Preston Dickinson and in short poems by William Carlos Williams. He and Hemingway make the most of lean verbal means. Their sentences and phrases strike a precarious balance because a failed plain style collapses more quickly than a shaky grand style. James Agee, for instance, rarely knows when to pass up proverbial butter and syrup in *Let Us Now Praise Famous Men*, though he usually manages to elevate the vernacular object in question, notwithstanding his Latinate vocabulary, which may be balanced or toned down by the presence of the plain-style photographs of his collaborator, Walker Evans. They celebrate humble kitchen utensils together in very different voices.

The Apotheosis of
the Vernacular

Louis Lozowick's high regard for his appetizing spread is marked by the way he implanted his branding-iron monogram in the lower left corner of the tablecloth (p. 127), making it a personalized setting by way of Gris's breakfast table (p. 79). Nourishing fruits do indeed cast a giant shadow, in the vernacular sense of the phrase, in Hemingway and Williams. Although typographical play doesn't figure in this 1916 photograph by Paul Strand (p. 131), the exact and arbitrary placement of words on a page does play a central role in Williams, whose seemingly artless verse is now in the spotlight.

Williams's short poem "To a Poor Old Woman" (1935) quickly evokes the title character, who is out on the street, munching and sucking plums from a paper bag:

> *They taste good to her*
> *They taste good*
> *to her. They taste*
> *good to her*

writes Williams in the second stanza. (Paul Strand was the first American to photograph such people close up.) The repetition of the simple phrase renders the consciousness and rising pleasure of the poor old woman, who wouldn't use "writerly" adverbs, adjectives, or tropes. The poet mines the full connotative depths of the plain words by varying the typographical placement of the repeated words. *Her, good,* and *taste* are thus treated to the pride of place of the right edge of the poem and all that blank margin—analogous to the open air of gallery space, where the three words, polished by repetition, can catch and hold the light, like a sequence of small Brancusi bronze eggs and glittering newborns displayed atop three neutral white pedestals. The only possible irony here is the need or urge to use high-flown metaphors to explain the audacious simplicity of Williams, any one of whose poems would collapse under the weight of a word such as *apotheosis*.

The virtual absence of end-stops in "To a Poor Old Woman" dispatches the fresh fruit home, special delivery, and floats it before us in an open-ended celebration of consciousness and elemental renewal:

> *a solace of ripe plums*
> *seeming to fill the air*
> *They taste good to her*

writes Williams in the fourth and final stanza. Paul Strand's pear is also as bright as a Brancusi and seems to extend beyond the picture plane, into the psychic space of the viewer, another way to bring home the taste and solace of fresh fruit. In Hemingway's best story, "Big Two-Hearted River" (*In Our Time*, 1925), a deeply troubled Nick Adams is rejuvenated by therapeutic physical challenges followed by delicious apricots. Pop art has canned such sweetness — in the vernacular sense of the verb, alas. It's been difficult for post-Pop artists and writers to bring it back.

If the essence of Williams's poem could be captured today in an irony-proof painting (e.g., the fruit in the "folk art" photographed by Walker Evans), it would deserve an ornate frame but look better in a plain one, like the border on Puni's *Baths* — the kind of frame now in favor at the Museum of Modern Art, where the elite meets the vernacular, even in the august Permanent Collection, on the second floor, where two folk paintings are on display, by Joseph Pickett and John Kane. In *Manchester Valley* (c. 1918), Pickett the unself-conscious naïf easily manages to express his love of country and high regard for education by painting the scene's country schoolhouse out of scale, looming above everything like a downtown department store, its mammoth, four-square American flag as large as one of the buildings in the foreground of the picture. Is it possible for a sensible, modern fellow (self-conscious, irony at the ready) to write in the first-person in praise of a public institution without embarrassing himself? Only the brave dare enter. "*Put up or shut up!*" shouts an old woman from the street, tossing an empty paper bag into the gutter near my feet.

Paul Strand, *Still Life, Pear and Bowls, Twin Lakes, Connecticut,* 1916.

The Museum

THE TYPOGRAPHICAL PLAY SEQUENCE culminates here, on the fourth floor of the Museum of Modern Art, in the entrance gallery of its Department of Architecture and Design, the most spectacular new area in the enlarged museum that reopened in 1984. This twenty-four-foot-high exhibition space, the highest in the museum, should be imagined as two walls in a utopian city where only the most handsome commercial art is posted, in frames, where it remains safe from the elements, thanks to protective glass. The Löwenbräu poster from "A Guide to Berlin" should be up there, too, if only out of deference to the story's elegiac narrator, who wants to rescue the city. (His use of the present tense has preserved it in one dimension.) "The streetcar will vanish in twenty years or so," he predicts, accurately. In 1945, twenty years later, a vast Soviet army destroyed much of Berlin. The narrator imagines a twenty-first-century "museum of technological history" that would preserve such "trifles" as streetcars, which anticipates both the National Air and Space Museum and the Smithsonian's National Museum of American History, where antiquated trolleys are indeed preserved. The latter wouldn't pass the admissions test at the Museum of Modern Art, where a car and helicopter are on display, and examples of commercial wallpaper are framed, but only because their design is first-rate.

The museum's pristine white walls (a radical choice in the thirties) and 1984 replacement of all ornate frames in favor of plain ones fulfill the intentions and example of Mondrian, who often mounted and encased his own compositions in white frames that were designed as protective, tranquil zones that would neutralize or minimize the discordant presence of adjacent works and ill-colored walls in the picture's next setting, an uncontrolled environment. The grandiose "frame" adorning the poster on the museum's right-hand wall (opposite) is illusionistic, and not a curatorial lapse in taste. It looks back to the self-reflexive equipoise and humor sustained by the "framed" pictures of Puni and Picasso. This poster is actually a unique and faithful tapestry duplication of the original version, a 13' × 15' 7 ½" lithograph, which was designed in 1935 by the

Entrance Gallery, Department of Architecture and Design, Museum of Modern Art, New York, 1984. The car, a Cisitalia "202" GT, was designed in 1946 by Pinin Farina. It is the first automobile to have entered the collection of an art museum.

most gifted graphic artist of the day, A. M. Cassandre, for Nicolas, a large Paris wine merchant. The artist depicts an old delivery man, a figure out of Atget, c. 1910, who here bears a stylized garland of wine bottles in each hand as he makes his daily rounds at sunrise, it seems, to judge by the shadows and Delaunay-inspired solar disks around him (yellow and peach are their principal hues). Cassandre's frame honors old Paris along with the grape (the man's "nimbus" is purple and green), and flatters the merchant, who surely didn't turn many ads into woven tapestries for the office. The elaborate frame is also comically inappropriate for an outdoor commercial locus, and Cassandre has slyly signed his name on the field of the image rather than anywhere on the "frame" to stress its (mock) fine arts status and, like Walker Evans's anonymous limner (p. 117), his own self-respect as an artist. Created only a year after the Museum of Modern Art had expanded the Department of Architecture to include Design,

Cassandre's poster seems to be saying, with a sunny wink, "Hey, I'm framed and ready for your Collection! Modernism for the Masses—a Utopian Dream! Someone propose a toast."

Alfred H. Barr, Jr., the museum's great first director, did all he could to realize the dream of a democracy of quality that would override traditional and snobbish distinctions between high art and low crafts. The influence of Alfred Barr is felt everywhere, from books that take Hi-Way Taverns seriously to indiscriminate enthusiasms at his own museum (e.g., a c. 1985 retrospective of James Bond films, posters included, which, if you take their content seriously—affectless mayhem as fun, nihilism for the masses—is the antithesis of the sensibility that Barr brought to bear on "high" and "low" forms alike. He did not wish to discard standards).

While in Europe in 1927–28, the year before his museum opened, Barr visited many of the artists, architects, and stage and film directors who believed most passionately in the idea that an improved and unified visual culture could only lead to social improvement and the self-renewal of ordinary citizens. He was much impressed by the Russian Constructivists, including Rodchenko, and the filmmaker Sergei Eisenstein; the Dutch De Stijl group, Mondrian among them; and especially the Bauhaus in Germany, where Paul Klee taught. "A fabulous institution," Barr later wrote of the short-lived Bauhaus (1919–33), soon to be closed by the dystopian Nazis. "Painting, graphic arts, architecture, the crafts, typography, theatre, cinema, photography, industrial design for mass production—all were studied and taught together in a large new modern building. . . . Undoubtedly [the Bauhaus] had an influence not only upon the plan for our Museum . . . but also upon a number of its exhibitions."

The Museum of Modern Art's 1938 show "Useful Household Objects under Five Dollars" was clearly a Bauhaus-induced production, the first in a series that aspired to teach the American public that inexpensive industrial items could be well designed and that everyone should keep an eye out for them. Several of the objects on view in the display case here (p. 133), photographed in 1984, had been in the 1938 exhibition, including the round steel tray. The largest object in the display case is a quite wide 1943 propeller blade that, aptly enough, looks like a Brancusi bird or some kind of tribal shield or ritual piece (see Lewis's painting, p. 18). But is the resemblance really apt and meaningful? Brancusi fashioned a complete array of household items out of poverty and his deep urge to create an organic, integrated "tribal" environment. Can we say that admirably designed useful objects bring any deep satisfaction to us? The

"American Modern" dinnerware, glazed earthenware designed in 1937 by Russel Wright. This array is from *The Machine Age in America*, a 1986 exhibition at the Brooklyn Museum.

aluminum bodied 1946 Cisitalia "202" GT car now on museum display is compelling and worthy of celebration because it is so clearly designed to move through space as smoothly as possible, everyone's ambition. We're in its skin, even if we're indifferent to cars. "I've got wheels," fifties slang for having a car, is apt; we like Brancusi for the same reason, and anthropomorphized vehicles in books for children. Rodchenko's "Comrade object" comes to mind. But does the day begin much better if our pancakes are served on an award-winning plate? Does coffee, wine, or beer taste any better if your good-looking glassware coheres with other parts of the room, everything designed in the utopian spirit or literal style of the Bauhaus, De Stijl, or any one of several Russian manners? (The striking porcelain of the Soviet agitprop artist Nikolai Suetin is on display, and reproductions of it are for sale in the museum gift shop.) Is it possible that an adult, eating a meal off a vivacious "classic" modern plate, can feel anything approaching the pleasure supposedly experienced by an original inhabitant of one of those utopian households? Or the felicity enjoyed by a child who's just polished off his or her food and watched the faces of Mickey Mouse and Pluto come into view again on the glorious clean plate? Isn't it ironic that the museum frowns on Art Deco as an eclectic style, even though the biomorphic and aerodynamic (Brancusi-derived? Arp-inspired?) mass-produced dishware of a Russel Wright (p. 135) may be as pleasing as that 1946 car? Do the people who collect classic modern plates ever actually *use* them? Does one's use of the rhetorical question and the impersonal pronoun disguise one's uneasiness with the subject, a fear of sounding effete about dishware? Why doesn't the Design Collection have any beer mugs on display? Is the form art-proof by definition? Is some wine-bound snobbery at work, even in utopia?

But whatever it is you want to see at the Museum of Modern Art, there's little chance that the crowds will part long enough for you to enjoy or contemplate it quietly, and for more than twelve seconds, unless you take advantage of Mondays. All New York City museums and private art galleries are closed on Monday except for the Museum of Modern Art. Because many people forget this or assume that it's closed, attendance is lighter that day. If you're there on a Monday when the museum opens at 11:00 A.M. and rush ahead of the modest assembly, you can have the inner galleries of the Permanent Collection on the second floor pretty much to yourself for about twenty minutes (people tend to view rooms consecutively, tourists in particular).

If you are lucky enough to visit the museum on a Monday when the weather is inclement, you may experience museum bliss, as I did a few years ago during a blizzard. I went directly to the spacious and empty Matisse gallery, one of the few rooms that is softened by natural light and comfortable benches. Instead of examining the pictures up close, one by one, in the manner of a museumgoer, I sat down in a cushioned, recessed seat beneath a window, and as alone as Robinson Crusoe before the arrival of Friday, I leaned back and gazed at the dozen or so large, sublime Matisses on the walls around me, especially *The Moroccans* (1916), with its spherical yellow and green melons in bloom (they could be supplicants in prayer), and the huge *Dance* of 1909, a rehearsal for *The Dance* of 1910 (p. 15). Twenty or thirty minutes must have passed. The gallery remained empty and silent. The place became mine. Could Nelson Rockefeller have felt as euphoric before his collection? In fact, *Dance* used to be in Rockefeller's living room, and he donated it to the museum in honor of Alfred Barr. A guard wandered in, and I wanted to send him out to get

An installation view of *Machine Art*, the 1934 exhibition directed by Philip Johnson that initiated the Museum of Modern Art's Design Collection. Almost everything is on a pedestal, as though they were Brancusis, which makes them and the
room look silly and pretentious now, like an adjunct to one of the vast, all-white
futuristic sets in the movie *Things to Come* (1936), a high-gloss adaptation of
H. G. Wells's book. Noteworthy examples of design are not always as deathless
as, say, works by Brancusi and Matisse, which doesn't mean that such objects
can't be converted easily into valuable coin. If the far-left side of this installation
shot was cropped to include the coils alone and then was reproduced here under
the taxonomic caption "Claes Oldenburg, *Slinky Toys: Model for a C.I.A. Monument,* 1969," you know you'd believe it. We've trusted the museum, its taste and
commitment to high standards in every department.

me a croissant and cup of coffee — no, let's make that wine, for two. But
the connoisseur and guard should meet as equals here, in this utopian
place, so I'll get the wine — or should it be beer? On the way out I'll pause
before the museum's version of Brancusi's bronze *Bird in Space*, notice
myself reflected in its polished surface, and wish that I could leave a Van
Eyck-like message on its base, in pencil.

The City Regained

FERNAND LÉGER'S large 7′7″ × 9′9″ painting *The City*, of 1919 (opposite), is a grandly optimistic if not utopian construct that looks even greater if you're familiar with his circumstances. The artist had served for four years in the recent war (1914–18) as an infantryman on the Argonne and then as a stretcher-bearer and sapper at Verdun. He was badly gassed there in 1916, toward the conclusion of the war's longest battle, where 700,000 men were killed and wounded on both sides during a nine-month period. Unlike Grosz, who formulated his outrage and despair (p. 61), Léger returned from the war to create a supremely serene city and the Africanesque drop curtain, set, and costumes for Milhaud's 1923 *ballet nègre, The Creation of the World*. Its text was written by Léger's life-long friend the poet Blaise Cendrars who had lost an arm in the war and then immersed himself in the study and translation of African literature and lore, out of which grew his *Anthologie nègre* (1921) and *The Creation of the World*, a story based on African creation myths. "Under the aegis of three Negro gods twenty-six feet tall [designed by Léger], one witnessed the birth of men, plants, and animals," Léger said in 1925, the year that Josephine Baker became the Afro-Cubist goddess of Jazz Age Paris. Viewers of such Léger postwar works as *The Cardplayers, The City*, and *Three Comrades* can witness the rebirth of Léger. The African god on the left of his 8 ¼″ × 10 ⅝″ design for *The Creation of the World* (p. 140) has only one arm (perhaps an allusion to Cendrars) but nonetheless manifests basic rebirth equipment such as a "lower torso" that is at once a tribal drum and a community cup. By basing many of his designs on schematic drawings and photos in ethnologic texts, Léger avoided the stereotypes of Parisian cabaret negritude. (His designs for *The Creation of the World* and the ballet *The Skating Rink* are generously reproduced, in color, in Bengt Häger's *The Swedish Ballet* [1990], a volume for the Twentieth-Century Celebratory Shelf.)

Léger's strongly vertical stage setting for *The Creation of the World* blended "primitive" motifs with the black silhouettes of tall city buildings (not in the preliminary pencil drawing included here), all beneath a be-

Fernand Léger, *The City*, 1919.

nign, rolling sky — a reversal of Conrad, whose *Heart of Darkness* draws civilization and the jungle together as one fallen world. The machinery of war notwithstanding, Léger had not abandoned his confidence in technology as the principal progressive force in modern life. Industrial motifs would dominate his work of the 1920s. The two cylindrical figures in the foreground of *The City* are an impersonal vision of efficient modern man, his path and person smoothed by technology. They should not be confused with the science-fiction automatons in Karel Čapek's play *RUR* (1920), Fritz Lang's German film *Metropolis* (1926), or any of the alienated, robotlike humanoids who appear in many other German works of the twenties. The illusionistically modeled gray spheres rising at the center of *The City* match the face of the foreground figure and are pleasing enough in their abstract, illegible way; in other Léger pictures, such modeled spheres clearly represent trees, fruit, clouds, and the breasts of

Fernand Léger, study for the decor of *The Creation of the World:* ballet by Blaise Cendrars, music by Darius Milhaud, choreography by Jean Borlin. Produced by the Ballets Suédois, Théâtre des Champs-Elysées, Paris, 1923.

full-figured women, which means that Léger's metallic, mechano-morphic sheen should be read as organic. The green vertical at the center of *The City*, a budding Maypole, stands for growth and hope of all kinds, as green so often does in the symbology of Matisse, Derain, Chagall, and Léger's friend Jean Hélion, whose capacious 6′6″ × 4′9 ⅛″ *Île de France* of 1935 (opposite)—a veritable marriage of Léger's and Calder's sus-pended shapes—appears early in this section because its application of Léger's mechanomorphic mode blends the city, countryside, and ocean. To see it this way, an American viewer must know that the actual Île-de-France is the geographic and cultural center of France, including as it does Paris, Chartres Cathedral, and the great châteaus of the Loire Val-ley, "the garden of the kings." Hélion omits the customary hyphens in his title to evoke, too, the name of the *Île de France*, France's grand Art Deco ocean liner, a fact that turns the composition's blue "sky" into a smoke-

Jean Hélion, *Île de France*, 1935.

stack above several deck funnels — part of a highly stylized stage design for a 1930s musical about happy voyages, featuring Maurice Chevalier rather than Josephine Baker in, say, a French version of Cole Porter's *Anything Goes* (1934).

The intentions of a Léger or the mechanomorphic Hélion (he had many styles) may be misunderstood today, so many antiwar years after the fact of their epoch's wide-ranging enthusiasm for technology. The 1937 Exposition Internationale in Paris and New York World's Fair of 1939 and 1940 would mark the zenith and conclusion of the Machine Age, as total war arrived. Delaunay's vast, brilliantly colored airplane murals in Aviation Hall at the Paris Exposition (produced with his wife, Sonia, an equally fine painter) were "answered" simultaneously in the Spanish Pavilion by Picasso's "newsreel"-hued air raid mural, *Guernica* — *Yes/No* in the context of putative entertainment. Yet the evolution of terrible weaponry should not render machine celebrants naïve and passé today, unless one discounts the recent achievements of technology, from

Fernand Léger, *The Cardplayers*, 1917.

computers to CT-scanners and pacemakers. And whenever such useful objects are handsome enough, the Architecture and Design Department of the Museum of Modern Art will display them. In 1988, a "Design for Independent Living" exhibit featured wheelchairs and prosthetic devices. For Léger, technology is renewal and harmony and strength, even if it must be perceived as metaphor or metonymn.

Witness Léger's large, easily misunderstood painting, *The Cardplayers*, 4′ × 7 ½′ (above). On the back of the canvas is the inscription, "Made in Paris on sick leave, December 1917." The title characters, three soldiers relaxing in a dugout at the front, are a robotlike mélange of ungainly but not grotesque machine-made parts that pay tribute to the metal, if you will, the fortitude and unyielding camaraderie of beleaguered men. Their large arms — cold, tubular steel, it seems — are hinged in such a way that they look as vulnerable as flesh and blood appendages — like the Tin Man in the *Oz* books or the famous 1939 film, whose "Yellow Brick Road" (music by Harold Arlen) is not irrelevant here. The cardplayer on the left of the picture has no fewer than four arms, Futurism's way of implying movement, and a soldier-artist's rueful addition of useful spare parts. Shortly before he was gassed, the thirty-five-year-old Léger had refused a chance to return to the rear to paint camouflage. He said he didn't want to leave "the boys," a locution we might find laughable if expressed in an old war movie or patriotic pulp story. Léger's populist sentiment is one with his machine aesthetic. His cardplayers are ennobled by the care with which he has shaded and modeled their metallic limbs.

Like Nabokov's anthropomorphized street pipes, with their "orifices," the humanity of Léger's machine-men shows through, quite literally. The metal tunic of the central cardplayer is open, revealing a raffish, red-and-white-striped jersey redolent of boatmen and cabaret dancers. It matches the red steps on the left, which also represent a backbone. The central cardplayer may be the ranking sergeant there (he's got three stripes on his steely sleeve and a medal on his chest), but at heart he's a citizen-

André Kertész, *In a Bistro, Paris,* 1927.

soldier rather than a Futurist's perfect fighting machine. He's also smoking a genteel pipe, probably to evoke *The Card Players* painted by Chardin and Cézanne, which makes him a genre subject in art history and part of the French tradition as well as a *poilu* — a "grunt." Civilization is not dead. Armor is only skin deep. Léger's machine-made men must not be confused with the bitter spirit and substance of Otto Dix's famous painting, *Cardplaying War Cripples* (1920), though it can happen, especially if Léger's picture is reproduced in deadening black and white, as it often is. Newsreel or newsprint monochrome is true to Léger's experience of war ("Four years without colors," he said) but the absence of color deprives *The Cardplayers* of its *élan vital*, from the red "vertebrae" and bluish tint of the limbs (the color of actual French uniforms) to the bright yellow of the soldiers' brick road gameboard. "They know that Hamlet and Lear are gay; / Gaiety transfiguring all that dread," wrote Yeats in "Lapis Lazuli" (1938), on the eve of another war. Of all the artists who served at the front in World War I, only Léger, the Englishman David Bomberg (another former sapper), and the Hungarian-born photographer André Kertész offer any kind of affirmation.

Kertész's photo of three maimed war veterans warming themselves in an underheated bistro (p. 143), taken in Paris in 1927, shares something of the spirit of Léger's dugout and the pub of "A Guide to Berlin." The man to the right of the stove is reaching through his crutches. The second man from the left is missing his left arm but his dandified scarf and the nicely shined shoes of the unshaven man on the left document their self-respect and respect for their fellows. These are photographic facts, as solid as the furniture. The wooden leg quite rightly looks like a wine bottle. The tabletop on the right is as glossy as a dance floor, and the stovepipe is their Maypole — to demonstrate how anyone can reify an object in the spirit of Nabokov, Brancusi, or Léger, who would have painted the wooden leg green, proclaiming him *un veillard encore vert* ("an old guy still green" [fertile]). The arbitrary green of Léger's *The Siphon* (1924) turns a casual occasion into a rite (the glass of such siphons was clear). Léger keeps a cooler lid on *The City*, but his telephone pole still has plenty to say.

As a foregrounded, vernacular form, the domineering telephone pole works for Léger the way Christian iconography served Old Masters. Its illusionistic modeling alone identifies its importance as form and subject, the only pole in town. It runs from top to bottom and out of *The City*

Air King radio, 1935. Designed by Harold L. Van Doren.

(p. 139), the way telephones do. Its invisible lines of communication conceivably link everyone, just as the Eiffel Tower can be seen from so many
places in Paris, though some vantage points are better than others. The
artist distributes shards of the tower on each side of his city so that everyone can share the landmark simultaneously, and they truly did, because it
beamed radio messages to charter members of the "global village" and
warned off low-flying airplanes. (The shards also look like airport py-
lons.) Stylized, zigzag electricity crackles on the horizon (top right), Léger's version of the Africanesque and stepped Aztec temple motif that
would shortly dominate Art Deco (1925–40), extending from the tops of
buildings to the matching "Aztec" radios (above) on living-room tabletops. (The last phase of Art Deco, which is often called Streamlined
Modern [the dishes on p. 135] dominated its decade, the thirties, as no
single style has in this century, which may be why Deco "collectibles"
such as Depression dishware and radios are sought so eagerly as "Comrade objects" — a way to tap into a culture that at least *looks* more coher-
ent than our own and, thanks to picture books if not objects, serves as

another [restorative?] version of pastoral.) Léger's solid circles and stenciled letters are part of a general harmony (the city has no name) and
should not be taken as any kind of specific traffic or commercial information. The telephone pole is painted *fin de siècle* mauve or purple, the
hue and density of a shaded, intimate conversation, which is within easy
enough reach now, thanks to technology. Brancusi might call it a modern tribal pole. The solid white circle on the far right of *The City* could
be the knob on a great outdoor radio. In American art, Stuart Davis
would turn it on, full volume, and make his cities pulsate and sometimes
dance.

Forms may overlap one another in *The City*, but they are never rude,
as befits Cubism's *La Grande Jatte*. None of the colors is too loud, and no
forms or colors seem to render the noise of traffic, Futurism's domain.
The primary movement is vertical rather than horizontal, which is in the
interest of street-level civility. Ascending (apartment house?) windows
mean that *The City* is a good place in which to live. This upward surge
(we're already off the ground) recalls the work of two of Léger's friends,
Delaunay and Brancusi. Each is invoked by Léger, who was one of the
few people ever photographed by Brancusi in the *mise en scène* of the
sculptor's staged, elemental environment (p. 148). The Eiffel Tower's
Ferris wheel in *The City*, featured in Delaunay's *Cardiff Team* (p. 55),
is conspicuously massive and immovable here, a monument rather than a
dynamic diversion, more like a Brancusi than any Delaunay. The Ferris
wheel, with its hopeful green gondola, reminds the viewer that Léger's
hard-edged approach is not to be confused with the rainbow lyr-
icism of Delaunay, who depicted the Eiffel Tower so many times that he
would seem to have leased it for his exclusive use from sunny June to
September.

The City of Light is in fact often quite gray, and this well-kept secret
as well as Cubism's penchant for muted colors explains why Léger's yellows are so pale, especially his replication of Brancusi's sculpture *The
Golden Bird* (opposite) in the foreground of *The City*, on a commanding
pedestal above the two mechanomorphic figures. Léger has transposed
the "African-Aztec" motif of its limestone base to his horizon, and
trimmed the sculpture's head after the example of Brancusi's newborn
Little Bird, an image of birth suitable to the needs of any postwar city
(p. 41). The painter's "concrete" version of Brancusi's 3'1/16"-high bronze
of 1919 looks ahead to the "avant-garde" public sculpture of today, right
down to the recent "art furniture" of Scott Burton, a close student of

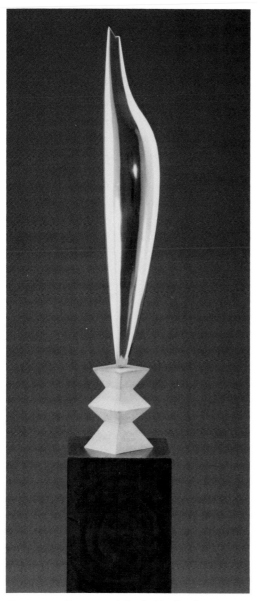

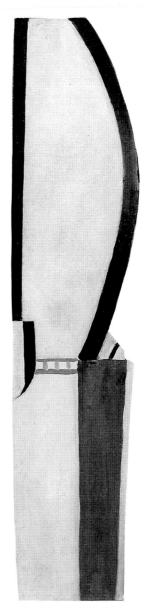

Constantin Brancusi, *The Golden Bird*, 1919.   Detail, Léger's *The City.*

Brancusi's oeuvre, who invokes the community cups of the master's Tirgu-Jiu war memorial in the granite tables and chairs he designed in 1985–86 for plazas in New York City, an excellent example of celebratory modernism as a daily presence in our lives (p. 149).

   Léger's "Golden Bird" confers dignity on *The City* and even *looks* like a dignitary. The mayor, if you will, is standing at attention, facing the pole, as though he's waiting to greet and salute the city's most recently honored and grandest public form, which seems to bear the two red bands of a double commander in France's Legion of Honor, awarded to the tele-

Opposite: Fernand Léger in Brancusi's studio, c. 1922. The conventional (fac-
tory-made?) chair looks particularly anachronistic in this elemental environment,
which seems to be recharging Léger's batteries. Photograph by Constantin Brancusi. Above: Scott Burton in 1986 with granite tables and chairs he designed for
plazas near Avenue of the Americas and Fifty-first and Fifty-second streets. The
hands of the artist, who died of AIDS in 1989, reverse Léger's pose.

Fernand Léger, *The Three Comrades*, 1920.

phone company and technology in general for services to the city and
nation. Could the red bands and dark stripe also be military chevrons?
This surmise is reinforced by the adjacent flat green image of an amputee
in silhouette. Its form is echoed by the one-dimensional silhouette suspended to the left of the "Brancusi," a bright red-mauve amputee whose
colors match those of *The City*'s lifeline and compositional spine. (Several
lifelong residents of Paris born between 1908 and 1910 assure me that

these silhouettes bear no resemblance to any traffic signs or public symbols of their day.) The striped or calibrated vertical on the second silhouette is its backbone, and it complements the vertebrae in *The Cardplayers.* Could the "doubling" of silhouettes be a reference to the ordeal and psychic rebirth of Blaise Cendrars, the re-creation of the world of the maimed poet? This would also make the silhouettes a reference to the return of Léger, who is always said to be a totally impersonal artist. The one-armed African god of Léger's fancy supports this line of speculation.

The overall harmonies of *The City* project Léger's peace of mind in 1919, while the two silhouettes look back to 1916 and the fragmented but still vital self that, after Verdun, had set out to find or regain the Perfect Place, a familiar idea from religion, mythology, art, literature, and popular culture (e.g., the Art Deco Emerald City from *The Wizard of Oz*). *The Cardplayers* of 1917 managed to add a dimension, literally, to the one-dimensional condition of the silhouettes, whose amputated arm must represent Cendrars's terrible wound. *The Three Comrades* of 1920 (opposite) could well be the demobilized cardplayers, immediately identifiable by virtue of the disembodied arm on the left, the pipe, and the triadic, magical number. Reading the 36 5/8″ × 28 3/4″ picture from left to right, we can watch a face come to life. The fellow on the left, such as he is, has a one-dimensional black-and-white head, and his sentience is represented by a garland of conical ear trumpets and little megaphones. Only his cane, with its egg-shaped knob, is fully shaded and modeled. The sole naturalistic force seems to have hatched from the two-dimensional ovoid at the center, who echoes the faces of the mechanomorphic figures in *The City.* This process of transformation is telescoped organically on the far right of *The Three Comrades*, where Léger has replicated some of Brancusi's egglike forms and, top right, dramatically positioned — as if in Brancusi's studio — an open-mouthed "sculpture" that conflates several of Brancusi's newborn babies and birds. Music from *The Creation of the World* should be playing now, to celebrate the arrival of the first naturalistic, human person in Léger's post-war oeuvre. *The City* could have been painted by this man, whose prosthetic hand suggests that the war is not entirely behind him. The *L* on *The City*'s telephone pole, a capital linkage (note the stenciled *F* to its left), is the initial of the implied fourth cardplayer of 1917, Léger's self-reflexive shorthand by way of the Van Eyck of *The Arnolfino Wedding:* "F. Léger was there [Verdun], and that's why this place is so splendid. Equipoise by the artist." The burden is on the self — to put the secular twentieth century in a nutshell (or Brancusi eggshell). "He was in his home where he had made it," Hemingway writes of Nick Adams in "Big Two-Hearted River," and he is only referring to an overnight pup tent. Nick Adams, traumatized by World War I (Kenneth Lynn wants to shift the blame to the author's mother), has come to psychic life again in the Michigan woods by successfully mastering basic tasks, getting everything right, happily, in striking and especially understated fashion when at the end of the story he cuts open his two freshly caught trout, producing "long gray-white strips of milt, smooth and clean. All the insides clean and compact. . . . When he held them back up in the water they looked like live fish. Their color was not gone yet." Not everyone knows that *milt* is the male reproductive gland of the fish. Anyone can see that these trout should be painted by Léger, Hélion, or Mondrian, milt alone by Brancusi.

If Nabokov's Berlin narrator were to pass Léger's three comrades and Nick Adams on the street (Nick would be wearing an old army tunic), he'd salute and greet them as brothers, and invite them for a Löwenbräu. Léger's 3′ × 2′ painting *Still Life with a Beer Mug* (1921–22), with its monumentalized mug (opposite), appears to anticipate such an event. Its high-pitched yellow rectangle is painted in the spot that's often occupied in landscapes and stage designs by an optimistic rising sun, while the white semicircle on the side of the beer mug echoes the ascending spheres in *The City*. The still life's other circles and spheres — all twenty-seven of them — demonstrate how Léger uses the symbol of completeness and Machine Age progress and transport (ball bearings, wheels, portholes) to raise his community cup higher, which is so big and heavy that it demands an industrial handle and probably two average-size fellows to hoist it when it's full — a community cup by definition. Léger's diamond-shaped floor pattern proposes a toast, picked up by the black verticals above them and reinforced by the legs of the two-dimensional table. The black and white squares also render movement — the hefting of mugs all around — and suggest that Léger's good friend Mondrian didn't invent *Broadway Boogie Woogie* out of the blue (or yellow). The table's stiltlike legs are an extreme example of the way Léger's picture-plane verticals often seem to run out of the frame, and down the wall, pipelining the picture's order and harmony into our grounded space. It even works on the printed page, though not as well as Kertész's Maypole photograph.

Fernand Léger, *Still Life with a Beer Mug*, 1921–22.

The richly modeled royal-blue curtain on the far right of *Still Life with a Beer Mug* is a deliberate anachronism that seems to define a proscenium, as though this were a stage and staged scene that, like *The Arnolfino Wedding*, has been set up very carefully to make a heartfelt declaration of solidarity: "*Salut!*" "*À votre santé!*" The men in the pubs and restaurants of *Ulysses* can be mean and piggish, and angry with Mr. Bloom when he doesn't buy them a round of drinks (they wrongly think he's won a bet), but Joyce shows without sentimentality that they draw strength from one another, from community. Solipsism doesn't rule their town, or Kertész's ordinary Paris neighborhood, where a bistro's shabby floor and furnishings serve to set off the uplifting shine on a man's shoes. "Cheers!" "Bottoms up!" — which is what Léger does, and says, with his diamond-patterned floor. If you down such a tankard quickly enough, you too can be green.

Sympathetic viewers of *The City* may wish that one of its coolly colored, interlocking shapes bore a CAFÉ or PUB sign, or at least a verbal fragment — a "FÉ" or "UB" — to suggest a warmer interior. A purely visual hint, such as a stenciled wineglass, would also be welcome. Only a desperate exegete would claim that the stenciled *R* (bottom left) is for "restaurant." But the form at the bottom left of *The City*'s "Brancusi" bird does look like another Brancusi-inspired cup, one better suited to hold Epps massproduct cocoa than beer or wine. It could also have served as a source for Scott Burton if he had wished to design a little row of outdoor wall extensions for the comfort of rush-hour plazagoers who are forced to consume their sandwiches and coffees-to-go while standing up. (Burton's death from AIDS in 1989 at the age of fifty is more poignant for the fact that he was an artist who truly wanted to serve the good of the public. The clenched fist and imploded left hand of the man in the photo state that he knows he is doomed, *The City*'s darkest silhouette in truth.) The great beer mug in Léger's *Still Life* is painted red, white, and blue, the colors of the French flag and, obviously, of that of their American allies in two world wars — Léger's cultural allies in matters pertaining to jazz, industrial progress, and the worth and welfare of the common man. "Hoist another one for the Yanks!" "Remember the fallen."

As German armies threatened France during the early months of World War II (1939–40), Léger thought about emigrating to America, and even made preliminary drawings for a mural that would celebrate New York harbor (opposite), especially the Statue of Liberty and three

Fernand Léger, Study I for *Cinematic Mural*, 1939–40.

ascending ship funnels (newly arrived from Europe?). There's nothing abstract about *these* Léger forms, Hélion's *Île de France* on a no-nonsense freedom run. The statue's vernacular symbolism was as attractive to Léger in 1939 as it would be fifty years later to the dissident students of Beijing, who in 1989 heroically paraded their Miss Liberty, or "Goddess of Democracy," an unpainted, hastily constructed papier-mâché conflation of France's *Liberté* and her American sister. "How *square*!" a hip postmodernist says of Léger's 20″ × 16″ drawing, choosing his slang deliberately from the Cold War period of the 1950s, when many sophisticated citizens, recoiling from McCarthyism, deemed our Miss Liberty an anachronism and ironic icon — *corny*, in a word, and I emphasize the epithet to celebrate its concreteness as metaphor. One can easily picture a string of dry husks suspended like pennants between Léger's middle funnel and Liberty's torch — a postmodern "appropriation" and send-up, the Spirit of '88, "Missing Liberty."

H. L. Mencken said that American slang is unusually vivid in its metaphors, a claim supported by Léger's most distinguished American compeer, Stuart Davis, who used all-capital and capitalized slang in many of his most densely packed major pictures, including PAD NO. 4 and THE MELLOW PAD — integral bits of free-floating writing that serve as titles, too. Pad means "homey apartment," of course, the subject and object of Davis's affection in a series of drawings and paintings that he produced between 1945 and 1962, only two years before his death. His pad had remained mellow, life was still a gas — you dig? "Solid, Jack!" says an eavesdropping jazz musician. At this point in a Davis abstraction, the artist might include a blue-and-yellow spade and the shard of a red gasoline pump, and hope that you can decode the hieroglyphics of Hip. The flag colors of *Still Life with a Beer Mug* declare quotidian life a holiday, like the "newspapers and magazines mounted on short staffs [that] hang like paper banners" at the end of "A Guide to Berlin," Nabokov's Christmas story. Form and color welcome us in Léger and Davis, which isn't always the affect of Cubism. "It don't mean a thing if it ain't got that swing," Davis wrote along the left-hand edge of his aptly titled *American Painting* (1932), quoting Duke Ellington's Cubist program.

The City and Town Pulsate

WHEN LÉGER visited Chicago and New York in 1931 and 1935, many American artists greeted him warmly as their master, especially in 1935, when the Museum of Modern Art mounted a massive Léger retrospective and *The City* was afterwards put on extended display at a New York gallery, where it subsequently influenced many painters, including Stuart Davis, who titled this 1938 mural *Swing Landscape* (p. 158). The "swing" refers to arranged, big band jazz, the best of which — Benny Goodman, Tommy Dorsey, Jimmie Lunceford, Charlie Barnet, Artie Shaw, Chick Webb, Duke Ellington, and Count Basie — constitutes the finest body of music ever to receive mass support in America (1935–46). Grouped together, the names of the band leaders swing — in counterpointed trochaic cadence, as it happens. A successful swing arrangement — with its call and response passages by the brass and reed sections, its solo breaks and rhythm "fills," its riffing choruses by the entire band — offers a paradigm for cooperation. As everyone knew, the fifteen or so fellows in a band lived and traveled together all year long, and had to get along, sometimes under arduous circumstances. The bands of Goodman, Shaw, and Barnet added black musicians long before major league baseball and the armed services were desegregated (1947–48). Their example was appropriate. The 7′ × 14′ *Swing Landscape* was commissioned by the Federal Art Project for the huge Williamsburg Housing Project near the East River in Brooklyn. Possibly the best government-sponsored mural of the 1930s, *Swing Landscape* represents Stuart Davis's hope that his "Colonial Cubism" (his phrase) could enhance daily life the way swing music did on the radio. (The leaders of the underground swing movement in Nazi Germany, who listened to American records in secret clubs, were eventually arrested and sent to concentration camps.)

Because it was intended for a Depression-era public space, *Swing Landscape* aspires to be more legible and openly cheery than Léger's *City*. The mural thus evokes many recognizable harbor sights such as various masts and rigging, a green ship's hull (center), and "the Williamsburg bridge" (left) — in quotation marks because a New Yorker and Brooklynite would

Stuart Davis, *Swing Landscape*, 1938.

quite naturally see it as one bridge or another while a resident of Gloucester, Massachusetts, would probably call it a Yankee fishing boat or schooner. Urbane Stuart Davis (he loved Bach as much as jazz and Checker cabs) spent every summer in Gloucester and the rest of the year in New York City. According to William C. Agee, the Davis scholar, *Swing Landscape* was painted in Gloucester (1940 population, 24,046). The composition seems to conflate town and city and two waterfronts in the hide-and-seek manner of a Joan Miró, whose visual conundrums and puns can make any landscape fun to negotiate. *Swing Landscape* calls for double takes, at least on the part of New Englanders and New Yorkers who want to deepen their focus. For instance, the two brown and black circular forms that help to anchor the lower left-hand corner of *Swing Landscape* could be chain links that are indeed part of a literal anchor (to see it the way a Gloucesterite might). But a schematizing city person perceives the "chain links" as sunglasses on the smiling, sun-saturated face of a happy (housing project?) resident, whose copper and yellow hues match Derain's sunniest jungle colors in *The Dance* (at least they do in the original paintings. Reproductions may be off). According to *The WPA Guide to New York City* (1939), "The houses [of the Williamsburg project] are placed at a fifteen-degree angle to the streets to orient the buildings toward the sun." The sunglasses of the cartoonish fellow (or figment) in the corner underscore such utopian amenities. "He" may also be smiling at a sunbathing female, and enjoying swing music, too, projected from an open window or two. Maybe Ellington and Basie are playing at the same time, on separate radios, their piano "fills" articulating the blacks and whites of *Swing Landscape*'s key color scheme.

Swing was disseminated most widely on the radio, which was free, of course. (Davis's blue-gray "harbor" is color coordinated with the Air King radio [p. 145], another utopian touch.) Radio music was aimed at dancers as well as listeners. It's easy to forget that "social dancing," as it was then called, was once a vastly popular communal activity (lessons were provided in junior high schools). "Live," nightly big band radio broadcasts from far-flung venues ("remotes," they called them) bridged continental gaps and helped to create or reinforce a sense of community and romance. Listeners could hear the dancers at a 1937 Benny Goodman engagement spontaneously sing and hum "Where or When" along with the band's strictly instrumental version. Maybe couples at home joined in, too; "Make Believe Ballroom" was the name of the most popular daytime swing-music radio show in New York City, presided over by disc jockey Martin Block, a name to suit town and city, and Léger and Davis, too. "Nothing connects," laments Eliot in *The Waste Land*. "'T'aint so, McGee," Stuart Davis says in effect — to draw on the famous vernacular tag line from one of the most popular radio comedies of the period. The promise implicit in *The City*'s dominant, personalized, mauve telephone pole shifts to lines of communication here. The various coils and cablelike forms in *Swing Landscape* (especially on the right) at once suggest the interior wires of a great radio, the fishing nets of Gloucester, and the maps in New York subway cars, the system that pipelined a good many Williamsburg residents to their work and weekend entertainment, too, in the area of Broadway and Times Square, where swing bands performed at vast ballrooms and movie theaters, at reasonable prices, and on the sound tracks of films such as Astaire and Rogers's *Swing Time* (1936,

Overleaf: Pearl Primus dancing to the song "Honeysuckle Rose" at an all-night jam session at Gjon Mili's studio-loft, New York City, 1943. Seated behind Primus are the jazz pianists Cliff Jackson (suspenders, bow tie) and, facing him, James P. Johnson. The band includes (from left) Lou McGarity, Bobby Hackett, Edmond Hall, Sid Catlett, Teddy Wilson at the piano, and John Simmons. Photograph by Gjon Mili. Copyright © Time Warner Inc.

music by Jerome Kern) and *Shall We Dance* (1937, music by George Gershwin). When Gershwin died in 1937, age thirty-nine, his last word was *Astaire*, which posits an attractive eschatology — a celestial swing landscape and literal state of grace.

Davis's entire composition can be said to outline the contours of jazz dancing, and of a place animated and colored by swing. Any interested reader can arrange and choreograph a *Swing Landscape* of his or her own by following these simple directions. First place a sheet of thin paper on Gjon Mili's photo of one of the many jam sessions that were held in his studio-loft (pp. 160–1). Ignore the section to the dancer's left, which is notable for the passive presence of the great jazz and ragtime pianist James P. Johnson, who should be playing at the second piano, in tandem with Teddy Wilson, "Jumpin' the Blacks and Whites" (a 1939 Wilson number). Now trace the outlines of the performers and their instruments, including the pianos. Then draw single vectors through the horns and along all oblique angles, top to bottom, in bold black, to achieve a Davis- and Léger-like network of lines and shapes (Davis was in fact a frequent guest at Mili's sessions, as was Mondrian). Next, you may use felt-tipped colored pens to saturate each outlined area with solid color, though this is an optional step given the fact that Davis's own monumental *History of Communications* mural at the 1939 New York World's Fair was presented as a black drawing on a white wall. But if you opt for color, the ovoids defined by the edges of Sid Catlett's two drumheads and high-hat cymbal must remain egg white, to echo the biomorphs created by Davis in the same section of his *Swing Landscape*.

Biomorphic forms quite naturally dot a waterfront landscape such as Davis's, from the black mastheads on the left — "fish eggs" or globes that have bobbed to the top as in a Calder mobile — to the white-and-blue ovoid (left of the green ship) that could have been pried loose from a Jean Arp painted wood relief and set free here as a fish or puff of smoke — "smoke," too, in the way that its essence, its taxonomic identity and "meaning," slips away. You cannot, you should not, pin it down too firmly. Biomorphic form must remain fluid to be affective, like Arp's *Human Concretion* of 1935 (19 ½″ high, 18 ¾″ wide), which looks like an embryo or fetus (opposite) that bears a bird's head (left) and baby's buttocks while casting the shadow of a gentle manatee or Miróesque Ur–Muppet in profile — the Muppet named Alf, I'm pleased to say. Davis's lobster-red "smoke" (top left) is also a whale by Calder, a cloud, a tree, and another Ur-Muppet in profile, its mouth open in song (Harold Ar-

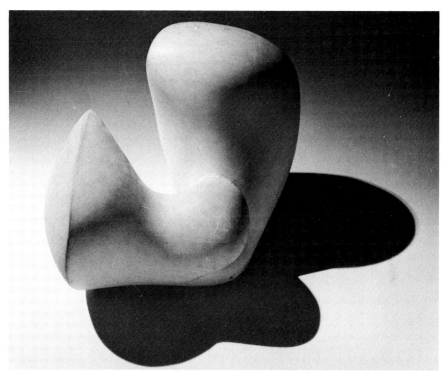

Jean Arp, *Human Concretion*, 1935.

len's "Get Happy," if logic rules). "They" are all drawn to the sun and sky by osmosis and a sense of pleasure, as are two of the four brown-and-blue biomorphic creatures at the top center — one of whom, in Arp-like profile (to the right of the pink-and-turquoise knotted figure), resembles some sort of fowl — a hep chick, to toy once more with 1930s slang or jive in the spirit of Davis. This chick, or bird, is on the alert, roused by swing and the distinct but distant sight of a potential meal: one of Nabokov's anthropomorphized Berlin pipes that has here turned into a biomorphic form (bottom right) that is either an inchworm attired in a thirties-style swimsuit or a caterpillar in the raw, taking its ease in the sun. If this were one of Walt Disney's *Silly Symphony* animated cartoon shorts from the thirties — *Music Land* (1935), for instance — the biomorphic pipe would stand up and sing and dance (Johnny Mercer's "Glow Worm"). And if these suppositions and the reference to the Muppets sound silly, then you don't understand the deep playfulness and open-mindedness of artists such as Davis, and Calder, whose sculpted crescent moons of the 1930s, especially in *Gibraltar* (frontispiece), surely ape the "sculpted" slices of moon in George Herriman's extraordinary comic strip *Krazy Kat*. Curators and critics worry such "crossovers" to death, which misses the point: the philoprogenitive essence of Brancusi, Miró, Arp, Calder, Davis, and jazz, where a hot soloist is free to quote *anything*, interpolating an incongruous fragment from another song in a way that gives it — and us — new life. (*Music Land*, by the way, featured a war between the Isles of Symphony and Jazz, which is ended on the Bridge of Harmony by the marriage of an anthropomorphized male tenor saxophone [jazz] and a female violin [a female form to the Cubists, of course, along with the guitar]. Disney enjoyed a good reputation in serious circles in the 1930s, not that this would have meant anything to Davis, even if you told him that *Swing Landscape*'s biomorphs constitute a perfect "high"/"low" fusion [Arp + Disney].) As for the worm that would glow, Davis's almost macaronic *Swing Landscape* is too crowded to tolerate any dancing creatures or automotive traffic; its colors are only allowed to jitter in place, joyously, as befits urban, town, and waterfront pantheism. Mondrian's *Broadway Boogie Woogie* (1942–43) would soon let swing rhythms loose, and jitterbugs, too. As in Léger, Davis's strong verticals and use of black and white temper and block any sense of movement in his town and city. The biomorphic pipe is in fact grounded fore and aft by solid black. But the black-and-white "egg" (to the right of the alert fowl) promises urban renewal. *Swing Landscape* is nothing less than a total gas. When the latter word appears in a Stuart Davis painting of the 1940s (with or without a petrol station), it has to be a punning homonym — urbane renewal, obviously, *New* York and *New* England. Dig it? "Solid, Jack!" "Yup, bub."

What does the pulsating, $4' \times 6'$ composition on the opposite page represent? It's by Joan Miró (1927) and is offered without any title or verbal clue for now. The picture is even more one-dimensional than Léger or Davis, whose *Swing Landscape* grows most difficult in its right-hand section. This third of the mural is almost entirely abstract, except for its shard of a ladder (not every viewer will have seen that pipe, or acknowledge its metamorphosis). It's a sort of painter's joke, a teasing space that hints at what the entire composition might have been like: Abstract Art, certainly not the people's choice in the 1930s, when corny Regionalist realism prevailed, particularly in mural art — and not the choice of Comrade Rodchenko and Davis, either, who both wished to communicate with the urban proletariat (Davis was in fact a Communist fellow traveler at this time).

The abstract "panel" on the right side of *Swing Landscape* (the position of Hell in old religious triptychs) could be a blueprint for one of the free-form metal or concrete open-air sculptures that have been erected in public spaces since the 1960s, the best of which (by Calder, Anthony Caro, Mark Di Suvero, Picasso, David Smith, and Miró) have been enjoyed or passively accepted by the descendants, as it were, of the Williamsburg project.

The Miró painting is titled *Landscape with Rabbit and Flower*. The sky is nocturnal, and the yellow rabbit smiles twice, thanks to the way its ears are paired — four smiles, really, since yellow counts as two smiles on the chromatic scale. Without Miró's title, a viewer might take the rabbit ears for a duck's bill turned to the right, or for any number of cartoon figures; one of my colleagues, born in 1957, identified the rabbit as the comic book creature Casper the Friendly Ghost (b. 1968). Miró's rabbit anticipates the famous 1939 "rabbit or duck?" visual conundrum with which Gombrich opens *Art and Illusion* (1960). A psychologist would expect or

Joan Miró, *Landscape with Rabbit and Flower*, 1927.

insist on an either/or choice. But Miró wouldn't find the forms mutually exclusive, or deny Casper; in Miró's more crowded landscapes, especially his farms, organisms seem to be caught in various stages of metamorphosis, as in one of those nature films whose time-lapse cinematography reveals ground zero as a hopping, fantastic place. (Recent microscopic photography and cinematography by Lennart Nilsson, especially his inside views of ovaries and wombs, confirms the accuracy or drift of the most "far-out" biomorphic creations. Arp's *Human Concretion*, for instance, could reasonably be said to represent the embryo of any number of creatures, in life and art, present company included.) Miró's "flower," a visual pun, is at once a blossom, an egg, a balloon, a half-moon, and a courageous spermatozoan on the move (only one in 125 million may survive), searching for his partner — playing his role, it seems, in a *Silly Symphony* or educational cartoon about the facts of life. "Where's Miss Egg?" asks the cruiser, underplaying the quixotic nature of the drama. Max Ernst's 1934 painting *Blind Swimmer* captures the tumult quite dynamically with its microcosmic view of a sperm shooting with the current past a stymied egg — one more near miss or mister.

The thinness of Miró's filament-"stem" facilitates and supports the multiple readings. "All" are elevated literally by the composition and exalted in space by the fact that the biomorph in question (there's one in the same place in Davis) is the only modeled, "raised," and sculpted form on a picture plane where pure color is celebrated even more openly than in Klee's "North African" *Signs in Yellow* (p. 91) or *The Dance* images by Matisse and Derain. This is an unrestricted *Swing Landscape*, an ideally flat, counter-Cubist ballroom floor for rabbits, who actually like to dance at night, in groups, particularly under moonlight. Sentimentality notwithstanding, the much-criticized anthropomorphized antics in Disney are not without factual base. But the tongue of Miró's rabbit is out, lizard- or serpentlike, which removes Disney from this picture. Miró's creature is alone, lest the artist's celebration of germination refer too overtly to the animal's reputation for sexual profligacy. (Rabbit mothers carry their babies to term in only six weeks and then are back on the street again.) As it is, the pairing of a rabbit and an egg-sperm-flower may be a less charming joke now than it was then because the *Playboy* bunny logo (b. 1954) and its offshoots have further sullied the rabbit's reputation.

Procreation is certainly no joke to Mr. Bloom in *Ulysses*, nor to Brancusi, Arp, and Calder, whose early mobile *The Pistil* (1931), 40″ × 12 ¾″

× 12 ¾″, is one of the first "serious" works that came out of his apprenticeship with his famous *Circus* (1926–31), the hand-animated toy big top that Calder, accompanied by phonograph records, presented to small audiences in Paris, where the avant-garde European artists welcomed the

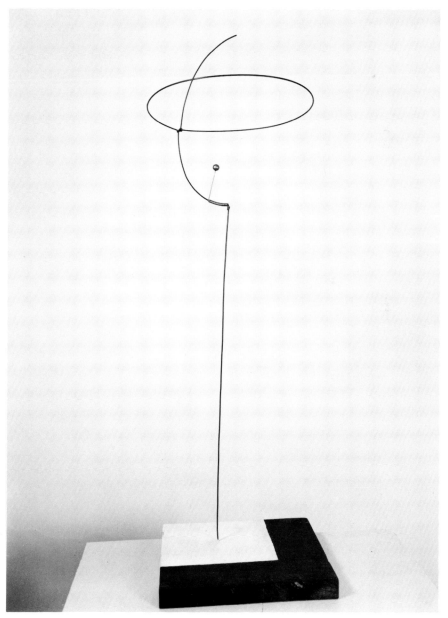

Alexander Calder, *The Pistil*, 1931.

expatriate American and his show as their very own *Silly Symphony* festival. Both *The Circus* and *The Pistil* (p. 167) reflect the influence of Calder's new friends in the neighborhood, especially Mondrian (who could have painted the wooden base), Miró, and Arp, the Paris pipeline at its best — direct, and literally economical (the mobile is constructed of wire and brass). *The Pistil* is a witty but not jokey depiction of another economical and efficient process, involving the male and female parts of a flower, and the possibility of self-germination, which does spare one the time, effort, expense, and stress of courtship (the author deliberately risks coyness here, trying to fix the tricky borderline between the charm of a Miró and the cloying aspects of even the best early Disney anthropomorphism). Ten percent of flowers are in fact sexually self-sufficient, and Calder's little (spermatic) sphere, bolstered at the joint by a coil-spring, looks as though it won't miss its target, the ovary looming above it. The wire ovoid or loop represents the pistil's ovary, in the highest spirit of biomorphism because it also traces a nimbus and planetary orbit. Calder's little sphere serves as a full moon, too, the best time for ovulation, many believe, including Leopold Bloom, though such "knowledge" hasn't affected or altered Bloom's sexually immobilizing belief that his seed is deathly weak. This little sphere points to the global "egg" of *Gibraltar* (frontispiece), which is incubating still — and is long overdue. Disney would proffer a bird father-to-be, pacing back and forth anxiously.

Despite its range, *The Pistil* may finally seem cartoon-simple and minor now — a clever offspring of Arp and Brancusi, whose influential biomorphic sculpted forms still represent a major, inspiring vision of the life cycle, starting with the egg, naturally. Brancusi's most famous egg (1920) is in fact a slightly asymmetrical ovoid rather than a perfect egg, so that when he photographed it on a shiny surface, the form and its twinned reflection suggested a range of organic possibilities, including a pear and a perfect pair of lungs and faces, the Adam and Eve of ovoids. This isn't fanciful. Brancusi titled it *The Beginning of the World*. The "female" plate and "masculine" shadows in Steichen's Brancusi-inflected photograph (opposite) herald human procreation, and a sequence of thirteen images that will culminate in the fantastic self-generation of Mr. Leopold Bloom, childbirth included.

Edward Steichen, *Pear on a Plate*, 1920.

Early in Art History

THE LOVERS, a 27 ½" × 46" plaster relief created by Raymond Duchamp-Villon in 1913, five years before his death in World War I, aspires to commemorate vanished lovers and epochs by "unearthing" and displaying this ancient "rock shelter" and "carving" of a totemic couple who, eroded and burnished by many millennia, have somehow survived (opposite). The female is on the left, and her triangular head, abdomen, and lower leg — archaeological fragments all — are akin to the triangular, almost featureless faces and pure forms of the marble statues of Cyclades, c. 2600 B.C., the earliest known sculptures from Greek lands. His head replicates a fertility amulet's, from Paros of the same period. His boulderlike shoulder and thrusting, phallic thigh defy time, in a "shelter" whose roof is shaped like an egg or ovary. These forms survive, in relief, to be contemplated by any descendants of the tribe who happen upon them.

In *The Sentimental Education* (1869), Flaubert describes the forest of Fontainebleau, where two Parisian lovers seek refuge from the upheavals of 1848: "The path zigzags between the stunted pines under the rocks with angular profiles; this whole corner of the forest is somewhat stifling, a little wild and close. . . . The rocks filled the entire landscape . . . cubic like houses, flat like slabs of cut stone, supporting each other, overhanging in confusion, like the unrecognizable and monstrous ruins of some vanished city. But the fury of their chaos makes one think rather of volcanos, deluges and great forgotten cataclysms. Frédéric said that they were there since the beginning of the world and would be there until the end. Rosanette looked away, saying that it would make her mad." Faced with such rocks, Lachaise would hug his wife and envision three or four future works. Brancusi would drag home a few of the rocks and use them, for a while, as photographic props in his ever dramatic and evolving *mise en scène*. An early modernist photographer (1915–30) who has been trained to see by Cézanne, Cubism, examples of tribal and archaic art, and possibly, too, the prose of Flaubert (e.g., Walker Evans), would unpack and set up his large-view camera and explain his intentions to his young female companion: "To photograph a rock, have it look like a rock, but be more than a rock" (as Edward Weston wrote in his posthumously published *Daybooks* [1966]).

Raymond Duchamp-Villon, *The Lovers*, 1913.

More Than a Rock

PERCEPTION, as everyone knows, is a mysterious process that involves physiology and psychology, memory and habit, and any concrete body of information you happen to possess. This photograph was taken in 1919 by Paul Strand, who simply titled it *Rock, Port Lorne, Nova Scotia* (opposite). Had he seen something definite and paraphrasable here to make him frame it this particular way? Our own perception of it is surely affected by its context. Duchamp-Villon's legible "rock formations" prepare and encourage us to find *trompe l'oeil* physiognomic configurations now. The largest wedge thus constitutes a female's abdomen, tapering into pudendum and flanked by Cubistic hips, which, on a second "take" or glance, turn into the hunched shoulders and arms of a rather bashful, long-faced woman who is being nuzzled by a triangular swain in Cycladic or Easter Island profile, a man of few words. Their eyes are closed. The example of Modigliani's sculpted, elongated "archaic" or "primitive" limestone heads of 1911–15 must have moved the photographer to search for such nascent figures. Their union defines and begets a tree, the *Y*-shaped "sapling" that rises up from the lower right corner. These forms seem to be metamorphosing before our eyes, and a metamorphosis can be a thrilling sight, as in Klee. Pan meets pantheism, snugly and solidly, effecting an eternal pair, if only in geological terms, since she really does look sad and he appears to be an oppressive load to bear, one that has grown heavier with each passing eon.

Fruits, vegetables, and pairs will dominate this sequence, if you can perceive the forms the way I do. "The Doubloon" chapter of *Moby-Dick* is apposite. The doubloon is a gold coin from Ecuador that Ahab nails to the central mast of the ship as a prize for the crew member who first sights the White Whale. Each of the book's main characters analyzes aloud the doubloon's inscrutable symbolic figuration, each seeing something different as Pip, Melville's version of King Lear's fool, describes their efforts and accepts the fallibility of perception and the impossibility of absolute knowledge. "I look, you look, he looks; we look, ye look, they look," he says. The reader should ask a random sampling of friends what they see in the rock. By the way, doesn't the "torso/head" configuration on the left also look like a manatee? "What's a manatee?" asks a stricken reader. The word was used once before in these pages, in regard to Jean Arp.

Paul Strand, *Rock, Port Lorne, Nova Scotia,* 1919.

The Flowering Pair

CERTAIN ARTISTS AND WRITERS force us to perceive reality in surprisingly sensuous or sensual ways, as when Brancusi conflates a pear and buttocks in his thirteen-inch-high 1922 *Torso of a Girl* (p. 177) and Nabokov unfolds the landscape of *Lolita*. "Voraciously we consumed those long highways, in rapt silence we glided over their glossy black dance floors," writes Humbert Humbert, describing his cross-country car trip with the twelve-year-old Lolita, his virtual prisoner. He remembers that, beyond the conventional tilled plain and roofs of the countryside,

> there would be a slow suffusion of inutile loveliness, a low sun in a platinum haze with a warm, peeled-peach tinge pervading the upper edge of a two-dimensional, dove-gray cloud fusing with the distant amorous mist. There might be a line of spaced trees silhouetted against the horizen, and hot still noons above a wilderness of clover, and Claude Lorrain clouds inscribed remotely into misty azure with only their cumulus part conspicuous against the neutral swoon of the background. Or again, it might be a stern El Greco horizon, pregnant with inky rain, and a passing glimpse of some mummy-necked farmer . . .

Mummy-necked, or elongated, as in El Greco, and essentially dead, because Humbert Humbert, consumed by obsession, has depopulated, eroticized, and aestheticized the visible world. Reread the passage and see how discreetly Nabokov manages to warm and impregnate the sky: "slow suffusion"; "fusing"; "swoon." These words also describe the actions of Georgia O'Keeffe's and Edward Weston's organic forms, if you perceive them as functioning bodies and bodily functions.

O'Keeffe's 1927 painting *Red Cannas* (opposite), a veritable *trompe l'oeil*, contains a (male or female) creature who is nuzzling a partner who must be female, given the breastlike tip of her docile "head." The form on the right is his (or her) gentle hand or paw. At a third glance, the form on the bottom left becomes a buttocks or ripe fruit of some sort, an apple-pear-

Georgia O'Keeffe, *Red Cannas*, 1927.

peach hybridization that could have been shaped by Brancusi in limestone, or limbstone (puns, you remember, are budding or flowering
biomorphs, depending on their size and potential for growth). The ambiguities pertaining to the sexual gender of these "creatures" are consistent with Benita Eisler's revelation of the painter's bisexuality in *O'Keeffe
and Stieglitz: An American Romance* (1991).

Topped by a single, seminal, pre- or postcoital "dew drop," the 38 ⅛"
× 30 ⅛" *Red Cannas* are more subtle in their eroticism than any of
O'Keeffe's better-known "phallic" lilies of 1923–28 or the flamboyant
Jack-in-the-Pulpit series of 1930, one of whose manly stamens even
seems to be ejaculating — a tapered white jetstream, flame, or fountain

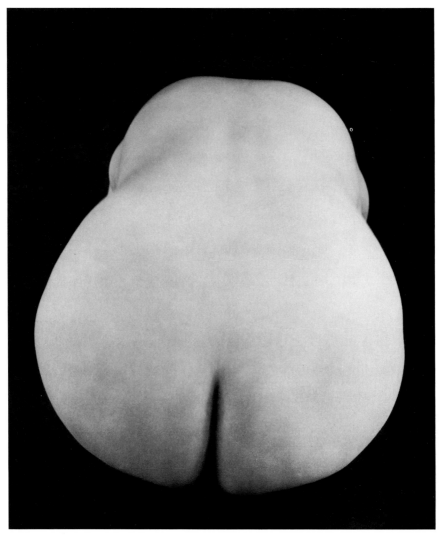

Edward Weston, *Nude*, 1925.

silhouetted against pitch black — the *Bird in Space* of ejaculations. This series was for its day a brave and outrageous attempt to answer the question: what does it feel like to have a man inside you?

> Yes when I lit the lamp yes because he must have come 3 or 4 times with that tremendous big red brute of a thing he has I thought the vein or whatever the dickens they call it was going to burst . . . no I never in all my life felt anyone had one the size of that to make you feel full up . . . whats the idea making us like that with a big hole in the middle of us (742)

Constantin Brancusi, *Torso of a Girl*, 1922.

So thinks Molly Bloom, contemplating her initial assignation with Blazes Boylan earlier that day. Contemporary feminists have taken exception to Molly's yearning and sense of awe, forgetting, it seems, that she and her husband suffer his dysfunction together. Her uninhibited and sometimes obscene turns of phrase formulate the extent of her unrealized needs and point to the central question of *Ulysses:* will she and Bloom ever have full intercourse again? And would such congress produce another bloom? A single, simple pun could conceivably constitute a long novel's "happy ending."

The Amorous Peppers

Edward Weston's photographs of peppers are often said to be erotic and ambiguous, though this pair (opposite) are caught at a turning point in their relationship that would inarguably give pause to the editor of a facts of life educational film. An art movie would point out that their polymorphous play and erotic posture (Bloom's favorite angle, too) seem to have been inspired by Georgia O'Keeffe's *Red Cannas* and biomorphic sculptures by Brancusi such as *Princess X* (1916) — an appropriate film rating — and *Portrait of Nancy Cunard* (1928), whose bulbous and elegantly twisted organic shapes belong on a family tree that includes more than one pepper, squash, cucumber, and male private part. Weston's photograph underscores once again the conventional opinion that the fine arts always anticipate and/or influence the work of even the best photographers. Russell Lee's debt to Stuart Davis and Gerald Murphy is a perfect example (p. 119), as is the pearing of the Brancusi and Weston female forms. Davis's Arp-like "chicks" are cozy in their *Swing Landscape* roost, whatever their artistic parentage; painters don't have to apologize, though "art photography" does. "Actually I have proved, through photography, that Nature has all the 'abstract' (simplified) forms Brancusi or any other artist can imagine. With my camera I go direct to Brancusi's *source*. I find *ready to use*, select and isolate, what he has to 'create,'" wrote Weston in 1932, annoyed by accusations that he had imitated Brancusi. But Weston transcends his artistic sources with peppers that are more compelling than this derivative 1929 pair. The delicate tracery of "capillaries" on the inside wall of Weston's white bowl, a womb for the nonce, suggests the delicate pulse of new life, and the possibility of artistic growth, represented here by a pepper Weston photographed in his California kitchen in 1930 (p. 181).

This smiling pepper constitutes a Rorschach test for all seasons. I see . . . I also see two seals nuzzling . . . nuzzling atop a dolphin (Brancusi, Arp, and Lachaise also sculpted seals and dolphins). You know this is a dolphin from the smile — the dolphin's natural expression, consistent with the fine character and warm disposition that have long made it an

Edward Weston, *Two Peppers*, 1929.

emblem of swiftness, intelligence, diligence, love, and divinity, and, to-day, a popular captive-performer at aquatic shows (it was a sacred animal in Greek and Roman mythology and a symbol of the gods and goddesses of the sea). At a third glance, however, a third seal appears on the bottom on its back, beneath the smile — *my God!* A seal orgy! The dolphin re-cedes, the "smile" disappears, and when it returns, it's no longer so sin-cere or benign. Derain's snake comes to mind, as does the smirk of Lewis Carroll's Cheshire cat. How long did it take Weston to find and pose such an O'Keeffe-like *trompe l'oeil* form? SEX-CRAZED SEALS SHOCK NATURE-LOVERS! proclaims the headline in the Sierra Club newsletter. The headline could be from the "Aeolus" chapter of *Ulysses*, where Joyce an-ticipates and mocks all cheap journalese, right through the supermarket tabloids of our own time. ANNE WIMBLES, FLO WANGLES reads the concluding headline of "Aeolus," in regard to the erotic deportment of two "frisky frumps." We don't know what those verbs mean, but they're as compromising and amusing as some of the antics of Weston's hot peppers — and no one has ever called Weston amusing before.

The sequence of pears, rocks, flowers, and vegetables that began with Steichen's photograph of genitalia (p. 169) does in fact capture the way any normal, unpoetic male or female daydreamer might anthropomorphize and eroticize reality in a matter of seconds, whatever the locus. These forms celebrate the morally brightest side of our guilt-free, natural sensuality: no one's been hurt, and none of these bodies is equivalent to the two dazed "initiates" in Derain's jungle clearing (p. 19). Everything is at a psychic remove, it would seem, like Weston's pear-shaped nude of 1925 (p. 176); Matisse's Odalisques; and young Lolita, in her first year with Humbert, when he believes he has "safely solipsized" his object of desire. Humbert is wrong, of course, and eventually says so, just as there is another current running through the ambiguous form of this pepper. The creature on the bottom also looks like it's being attacked, and may be in dire peril. A narrative threatens to unfold, and it's no laughing matter now.

Edward Weston had in fact deserted his wife, children, and commercial portrait business in early middle age to pursue Art and Free Love, a 1920s pairing. The two are personified neatly and broadly, and capitalized, the way our needs should be recognized and satisfied. But Weston's many peppers, seen collectively (thirty or so images), are at once celebratory and wrenching, registering an emotional torsion: passion and guilt, joy and despair, fulfillment and pain. Naturally contorted peppers are by definition better suited than smooth apples or pears to express the price of such a second life, if that's what they do: tell the story that Gauguin would not submit to his art. This line of analysis is of course heretical: visual form is not supposed to have content, but if you're innocent of dogma and dicta, the moral chiaroscuro of Weston's shadowy peppers should be keenly felt, "literary" as this may sound. Other Weston peppers (not pictured here, of course) are propped straight up, still on their feet, but terribly twisted and wrinkled, their sensuality and passion all dried up, their salad days over, regrets intact — so to speak. We may forget these are only vegetables, mere *peppers*, not sculpted forms. Their extraordinary subjective power has nothing to do with the stress-free perfectionism of Brancusi and Arp; or Weston's own Brancusi-like bare

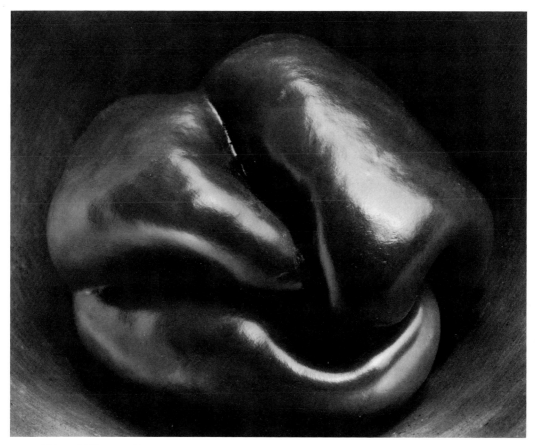

Edward Weston, *Pepper*, 1930.

trees, rocks, shells, and cold nudes; or O'Keeffe's brave but uncomplicated celebration of her flowering erotic nature. To see Weston's peppers
in this light is to celebrate unconditionally the art in "art photography"
(under attack as irrelevant), its complexity (the Derain comparison), and
to hold it up to a famous line in Yeats. In Weston's peppers, the dancers
and the dance are at once indistinguishable, and magically articulate: "O
Edward, let us up out of this, alive!" This biomorphic pepper would stand
a better chance in the self-generating world of Calder, Steichen,
O'Keeffe, and the "Nighttown" section of *Ulysses*, where Mr. Bloom
really flowers.

Gaston Lachaise, *Dynamo Mother*, 1933.

Dublin Man Gives Birth
to Octuplets

ALTHOUGH LACHAISE'S *Dynamo Mother* (opposite) is too bold to be called "ambiguous," it may still pose a perceptual challenge to impatient or bashful viewers. They might well miss the fact that the posture of this 1933 bronze celebrates procreation by conflating the acts of love and childbirth. The fetus has dropped, its head swelling the pelvis, allowing the raised vagina to define the infant's vulnerable fontanelle, the only "soft" spot in one maternal form that may be difficult to like at first wince. Its deliberately rough epidermis evokes the baked mud surface of a tribal fetish that is at once "primitive" and universal; the buttocks are nothing less than global (more so from the rear, p. 188) and support male as well as female parts. "Masculinity" is limned by a weightlifter's musculature and erect penile breasts and nipples, which Lachaise surely modeled after the example of the stylized, phallic heads of androgynous marble fertility idols that were fashioned in Turkey, c. 2700 B.C., and buried with the dead in order to affirm the living (p. 184). Lachaise gives these idols new life through *Dynamo Mother*. His *Floating Figure* (p. 4) also has its masculine, archaic cast, a bald head derived from an Egyptian portrait bust of a prince of the great Fourth Dynasty, 2680–2564 B.C. Such androgynous constructions salute the "manly" steel of certain women and acknowledge the psychological and emotional reality of a man's "feminine" side, including his transsexual (Bloom, in part) or pansexual urge to mother as well as father a child.

"O, I so want to be a mother," says Bloom, in the magical "Nighttown" chapter, a two-hundred-page play-within-the-novel whose parenthetical, detailed "stage directions" must be read carefully because they carry so much novelistic weight (some readers only skim them). A self-pollinating flower here, Mr. Bloom promptly *"bears eight male yellow and white children,"* writes Joyce in his stage directions. The lads *"appear on a redcarpeted staircase adorned with expensive plants. All are handsome, with valuable, metallic faces, wellmade, respectably dressed and wellconducted, speaking five modern languages fluently and interested in various arts and sciences"* (494). These metallic boys are related to the perfect Man of the Future who

Abstract-Schematic Idol, Turkey, Anatolia, Early Bronze Age I–II, Beceysultan type, c. 2700 B.C. Marble. 3 ¾″ × 2 ⅛″.

Opposite: Alexander Calder, *Chock*, 1972. Calder's abbreviation of the brand name is a one-word credo and polemic addressed near the end of his life (he died in 1976) to artists of the future (Jeff Koons would be one) who would minimalize or mock the pro-life stance of High Modernists such as Calder and Brancusi.

would be tooled by Brancusi (p. 147) and Léger in 1919, in *The City*. (*Ulysses* is set in 1904.) Their metallic cousin (p. 185), Calder's twenty-eight-inch-high assemblage *Chock* (1972), is the long overdue issue of the global "egg" on *Gibraltar* (frontispiece), Molly's birthplace too. The bird's Chock Full o'Nuts coffee-tin torso is intact, a canned symbol of three-dimensional new life and an art chock full of values opposed to the one-dimensional, ironic detachment of Andy Warhol's soup-can approach — chock full o' nuttin', Joyce would say, putting on a New York accent. Puns are philoprogenitive, delivering at least two words where there had been one, which is progress. Because *Chock* reprises (and prizes) a series of jaunty wire-and-can assemblages that Calder made as toys for his grandchildren in the 1950s, *offspring* is the operative word.

The future looks promising indeed from the comic perspective of Nighttown. Bloom is here proclaimed Lord Mayor of Dublin, the first one of Jewish descent. A two-headed octopus in kilts, identified as THE END OF THE WORLD, "*Whirls through the murk, head over heels*" (507), urging a Scotch dance upon a multitude that does get out of hand, though Joyce saves it in time from the pandemonium of Grosz's nightmare city (p. 61). The returns aren't in on the End of the World, but a Jew, Robert Briscoe, did in fact become Lord Mayor of Dublin in 1956, and his son assumed the title in 1988, a textbook example of the optimistic rules of comedy and democracy. In the context of modernism, Joyce has outvoted the anti-Semitic party of his friends T. S. Eliot and Ezra Pound.

Nighttown's phantasmagoria are authorial and self-reflexive (Bloom's dead grandfather speaks directly to Joyce). The smallest "throwaway lines" and comic particles can be significant. At Bloom's mayoral coronation, for instance, "*A fife and drum band is heard in the distance playing the Kol Nidre*" (480), the mournful prayer and melody recited on Yom Kippur, the Jewish day of atonement, proffered by Joyce as a Mel Brooks routine long before the fact of the movie *Blazing Saddles* (1974), where a team of black men who are laying a railroad in the desert are asked by a racist cowboy to sing a "good ol' nigger work song." They comply with a "doo-wop" rhythm and blues version of "I Get a Kick out of You," Cole Porter's anthem of high society effeteness. Joyce's comic anachronism makes a psychological point: Bloom has borne his foolish, groundless guilt for too long. "If it's healthy it's from the mother. If not the man," he thinks in the "Hades" chapter (96). Bloom's protracted Yom Kippur must be drummed off, exorcised, and it is, on the last page of the "Nighttown" section. A spectral vision of Rudy appears, age eleven, and the moment is very affecting. "Rudy!" exclaims Mr. Bloom, reaching out to him gently (609). But Joyce's stage directions describe the boy as a ludicrous and grotesque figure and constitute a rejection of Rudy's debilitating hold on Bloom, whose grief is now seen as excessive and morbid. Will Mr. Bloom read his creator's directions, so to speak, and return to Molly's bed in the fullest sense? Even the early "Hades" chapter suggests that he will. On its last page, Mr. Bloom literally and figuratively turns his back on the graves. "Let them sleep in their maggoty beds," he thinks. "They are not going to get me this innings. Warm beds: warm fullblooded life" (115).

"Yes because he [Mr. Bloom] never did a thing like that before as ask to get his breakfast in bed with a couple of eggs since the *City Arms* hotel" (738), thinks an astonished Molly Bloom at the beginning of her interior monologue as she lies in her warm bed well after midnight. Bloom usually brings Molly breakfast (see above, p. 77), and the symbolic import of his request is underscored by biology when Molly's own egg suddenly departs her: "O patience above its pouring out of me like the sea anyhow he didnt make me pregnant" she thinks (769), recognizing that the monthly inconvenience of menstruation constitutes a happy ending and a potential new beginning. "He" (Blazes Boylan, the stallion) hasn't impregnated her during their first and undoubtedly only coupling (she thinks he's a lout), and now Bloom will have "one more chance," as she characterizes it. He's lying next to her, head to foot (as usual), in a fetal position, and is omnisciently described on the page before the start of her chapter as looking like a photograph of "the manchild in the womb" (737) — a *photo* because it's scientific, documentary proof, an X-ray to ponder as we enter Molly's mind. (Such womb photographs were not produced until 1964.)

Mrs. Bloom clearly wants another child, and remarks "the four years more I have of life up to thirty-five no Im what am I at all Ill be 33 in September will I," she wonders (751), contemplating a woman's prime and, implicitly, final childbearing years, though no reader can doubt Molly's fertility, given the powerful surge of her body and unself-conscious spirit. She doesn't know offhand how old she is and, in forty-five pages of unmediated prose, uses only two idiomatic similes and one metaphor, "Flower of the mountain" (of herself), but only because her husband once called her this. (Two years later, in 1924, Lachaise titled one of his

Gaston Lachaise, *Dynamo Mother*, 1933 (rear view).

ample, reclining females *The Mountain*.) Molly's creator allows none of his customary authorial attention-getters such as parodies, all-capital headlines, musical notations, foreign words, or obscure allusions to compromise and impede the rich, full flow of her supposedly a-literary "deep-down torrent," as she calls it — a torrent that blends ocean waters, menses, and the amniotic fluid of a woman's womb. In Molly's unpunctuated, typographically innocent section everything elides, the essence of pantheism. The titles of recollected songs and popular books swim past without benefit of italics, and there are no apostrophes, of course. *I'd* becomes *Id.* If Molly were a biomorphic, spatial form, she would be all egg, or a symbolic womb, based on the Ivory Coast model (p. 22) — in either instance, the largest one ever sculpted, painted, crafted, or assembled, something on the scale of Calder's earth/egg of *Gibraltar*. The rare capital *F* of Molly the Flower makes her typographically higher than the mountain — "a real pistil," they'd pun in the West. How could a spermatozoan miss such a target? Max Ernst's *Blind Swimmer* comes to mind. Molly's wombmate, Mr. Bloom (Joyce would say it that way, he would, he would) only has to relax and act as natural and normal as most any other fellow his age (thirty-eight): "but of course hes not natural like the rest of the world," thinks Molly (745).

Anyone who read *Ulysses* in college many years ago most likely still remembers the effect of its final pages (sonorously read aloud by the professor) and the dirty parts of Molly's monologue (underlined by males for the benefit of their pals in the dorm or frat), especially her graphic references to Boylan's private parts and Mr. Bloom's intense anal eroticism (780). But no one will remember Molly's extraordinary *sang-froid* about the latter, expressed on the second page of her soliloquy, when she thinks of Bloom, "then the usual kissing my bottom" (739). "*Usual! Usual?*" says a startled, totally bemused young reader, who might resent a sermon here on the connection between love and equanimity, wisdom and secular sainthood. Readers then and now seem consistently to have overlooked or undervalued the evidence of Molly's tender love for Bloom. "I suppose," she thinks, "well have him [Mr. Bloom] sitting up like the king of the country pumping the wrong end of the spoon up and down in his egg wherever he learned that from and I love to hear him falling up the stairs of a morning with the cups rattling on the tray" (764). As for the bigoted and foolish Dublin pub crawlers among whom Bloom finds himself, "well theyre not going to get my husband again into their clutches if I can help it making fun of him then behind his back" (773). Remembering the death of their baby, she thinks, "we were never the same since" (778), which means, specifically, that Bloom has stopped fulfilling his husbandly duty. "Its all his own fault if I am an adulteress," she reasons, quite fairly (780). She feels no guilt about Boylan, her sole extramarital transgression that we know about (Bloom's oft-remarked list of her twenty-five "lovers" is a cuckold's fantasy, save for the name of her first lover, Lt. Mulvey). Unlike Nabokov, say, who makes Humbert admit his moral failure, Joyce lets Molly off the hook completely, in part because Joyce knows that it's his own fault, and *Ulysses* here takes a sharp, extraliterary turn, one that refutes the recent charges that Joyce is antifeminist and hostile to women.

Ellmann's biography of Joyce (revised edition, 1982) and Brenda Maddox's *Nora: The Real Life of Molly Bloom* (1988) show that Joyce drew on his life with his companion and wife, Nora, in creating the Blooms. In Molly's section, he manages to voice his profound gratitude to his rock of Gibralter, the woman who would put up with his impossible ways for thirty-seven years. (Perhaps Mrs. Edward Weston was lucky that her difficult husband went away.) "Id rather die 20 times over than marry another of their sex," thinks Molly, "of course hed never find another woman like me to put up with him the way I do . . . yes and he knows that too at the bottom of his heart" (744). Molly refers to several of Joyce's most unattractive habits and quirky acts (bestowed on Bloom, of course), including the pornographic and coprophagous courtship letters the sexually troubled young Joyce had sent to Nora. (They were withheld from the first three volumes of Joyce's correspondence and only published in Ellmann's edition of the *Selected Letters* [1975].) "I suppose there isnt in all creation another man with the habits he has," Molly asserts, and the ambiguous male pronoun suits Joyce/Bloom perfectly (771). Joyce is saying *mea culpa* and *thank you* to long-suffering, stoical Nora/Molly: *thank you for making me feel like a man, thank you for helping me bear this book.*

The self-reflexivity of *Ulysses* is hardly frivolous, though Joyce did try to make Nora (his potential reader) laugh by having Molly address the author directly, "O Jamesy let me up out of this" (769) — out of this torrential menstruation, that is, which she responds to here like one of those put-upon characters in a self-reflexive comic film or animated cartoon who looks at the camera and asks, "Have you ever seen such cruelty?" (a primly bonneted old woman says this to us in *Blazing Saddles* while she's being beaten up by two scruffy outlaws). Although Molly notes that their bed has clean sheets, she isn't too finicky about her period, and waits two pages before she gropes for a "napkin" (771). Some people might call this primitive (without quotation marks) and not mean it as a compliment. As for Nora, she never did read *Ulysses*. Does a dolphin know that it's been sacred, and that it wears a perpetual smile?

Molly Bloom (the symphony) is beyond gender, finally, as is "her" literary voice and "credibility." Who surges this well, or at all? Such a magisterial *faux-naïf* verbal construct can't be called "primitive," either, though

Gaston Lachaise, *Burlesque Figure*, 1930.

the word highlights the essence of her chapter, as does a comparison between Mrs. Bloom's interior monologue and Gaston Lachaise's indelicate forms. His most excessive and sometimes ludicrous late works — huge breasts alone, given a life of their own — are analogous to what would have happened if Joyce had tried to shape an omniscient, third-person view of Molly's all-embracing consciousness.

Lachaise and his art may have been saved by what Proust called "the cleansing, exorcising pastime of parody" — in Lachaise's instance, the self-parody manifest in his 24 ½"-high *Burlesque Figure* of 1930 (p. 191). A prototypical "Lachaise woman" is reeling, overcome by the pain and vertigo that usually accompany the sudden birth of additional hips and buttocks. "O Gaston, let me out of this," she could be thinking, as she sinks beneath this burden, the artistic fate of many Lachaise works after the triumph of *Floating Figure*. His ability to laugh at himself through burlesque may have released him to create at least one more masterpiece, *Dynamo Mother*, before his unexpected death two years later, in 1935, at the age of fifty-three.

As for *Dynamo Mother*, it's too self-consciously allusive, too calculated to be termed "primitive" without those qualifying quotation marks. Its dynamic breasts and appendages are angled as programmatically as the soaring skyscrapers in many works by Lachaise's New York friends, including Charles Demuth, John Marin, Georgia O'Keeffe, Alfred Stieglitz, and Louis Lozowick. *Dynamo Mother* is only 10 ½" high and 17 ½ " wide (from one outstretched fingertip to the other), a fact that could be stretched into a lecture on monumentality (the idea and illusion of) and its psychological or emotional roots. Lachaise had emigrated from France in 1906, age twenty-three, to marry the much older American woman who was the sole inspiration and frequent model for his oceanic female forms. Perhaps his cult of the wife makes *him* primitive, unless we know and possibly practice it ourselves — a yestern religion (Joyce's persuasion) that still doesn't have its church or apparent cathedral. Lipchitz's Gothic-vaulted *Standing Personage* (p. 49) could serve as a model for such a structure if the *Personage* was inspired by Mrs. Lipchitz, who in fact lived on after Lipchitz's death to complete several of his unfinished works.

The City Meets
the Cathedral Sky

Louis Lozowick's 1923 *Chicago* (p. 195) reflects the skies and ceilings of Mondrian, Derain, Chagall, and Delaunay. Orchestrated fully, yellow unambiguously celebrates new life and potential growth, though the picture itself is surprisingly small (22" × 17 ½"). The city rises before our eyes, propelled by the express-train thrust of the perspective, whose merging lines create a myriad of happily ascending arrowheads; the black avenue at the center serves as a silhouetted church spire. If the green wall of large black windows looks forbidding, it's only because it reminds us of one of our own municipal parking garages. The white patch on the left, another forerunner of *Broadway Boogie Woogie*, highlights Lozowick's bright pace (even his table [p. 127] was swift). The stream of windows that runs from the bottom to the center seems to be outracing the two cars of the train, which is so elevated that it doesn't need tracks. Its industrial-red hue, the color of steel, matches several other surfaces, a surprising twist, since we expect steel to provide the skeleton rather than epidermis of a structure — to anthropomorphize the scene the way Nabokov vivifies those exposed pipes as the "entrails of the street" at the outset of "A Guide to Berlin." The steel framework of the building-in-progress is sky blue, a pantheistic reversal, and the green walls are hopeful color fields. The industrial-red arches are at once vaulted ceilings in the Cathedral of Industry, a twenties shrine, and a Bridge to the Future — hortatory symbology in crayon that looks heavy-handed today. The one-dimensional "arrow" on the top right still flies, however, as an objective correlative for unnamed technological improvements in our own age, and timeless harmonies that defy notation, as in Mondrian, when we view him with more or less innocent eyes.

The polarities of Mondrian interpretation are defined at one extreme by the metaphysicians, who take their lead from Mondrian himself — the Theosophist who saw his geometric abstractions as equivalents of the perfected state of the next dimension — and, on the other side, the earthbound literalists, who read his more austere compositions as elegant, overhead evocations of the totally flat countryside of his native Holland, whose fields, canals, and massive, solid beds of red, white, and yellow tulips are laid out at right angles. For most of us, however, Mondrian's paintings only matter as "pictures" if they can stand on their own as uplifting objective correlatives for our need, our search for order, psychic ease, calm, and renewed strength. As it happens, there are two large, framed Mondrian reproductions on the corridor wall next to the chapel of the hospital near my house, where I once stayed for a month. The physical therapy rooms are two doors down from the chapel.

If we were in the position of Mondrian's "foregrounded" blue-based square (see p. 7) — a structure in profile, a fulcrum in every way — we'd be proud to be able to support the rest of the picture so splendidly. Mondrian's yellow partakes of Lozowick's sky, whose blue steel framework is in turn reinforced by Nabokov's hardy sky-blue Löwenbräu lion, who marks a watering hole for blue-collar workers. And if my universe scans right, writes John Shade in *Pale Fire*, "So does the verse of galaxies divine / Which I suspect is an iambic line. / I'm reasonably sure that we survive / And that my darling somewhere is alive," he adds, referring to his dead daughter, a suicide in her teens. You recall that Shade also imagines a hereafter where there will be "talks / With Socrates and Proust in Cypress walks." At this point, someone must be thinking, or saying, *yeah, fine,* I also like immaculate cities, and hot peppers chased by cold beer, but this abstract and semi-abstract stuff is a long way from the naturalistic observations typical of a Nabokov. The objection is well taken, certainly, though "A Guide to Berlin" has only been offered as a springboard — I thought I'd made all this perfectly clear. I thought I had. Why are people so literal minded? Maybe it's my fault. It must be. It is. The pipes are really a thematic gimmick. That's all. *My* therapy room. Yellow and blue blocks. The entire structure is shaky. "Say, Dad, are you still a pantheist?" asks my adult daughter, on a rare visit home, and she laughs sweetly, intending no harm. She's in a good mood; in fact, she's expecting a baby. "These fragments I have shored against my ruins," says Eliot near the end of *The Waste Land*, speaking through the persona of the androgynous Tirisias, the only voice in the final stanza that isn't a literary allusion or liturgical shard. Let's look at some more photographs. They won't lie.

Louis Lozowick, *Chicago*, 1923.

The Overview

THIS *View from the Berlin Radio Tower* was photographed by László Moholy-Nagy in 1928 (opposite), the same year that Renger-Patzsch published his collection of photographs, *The World Is Beautiful.* The overview reveals another optimistic arrowhead, defined by the conjunction of the building and ground in the upper-right corner. Snow has melted around the rim of the pavilion roof, forming an *O.* So imposing an *O* must stand for Otto, in Nabokov's Berlin story, and *order,* as it might be traced in snow or wet sand by one of our artists or writers, especially Joyce, who early in *Ulysses* dispatches Stephen Dedalus to the beach, to look for the "signature of all things" (37), and much later sends Mr. Bloom into outer space to get a better perspective on his "perfect day" (729). Fresh perspectives are the literal rule in almost every image of *The New Vision,* as Moholy-Nagy titled his influential book of 1930. Let's move quickly now, and watch the quotidian universe scan — headlined accordingly, as a fast-breaking tabloid news story.

László Moholy-Nagy, *View from the Berlin Radio Tower*, 1928.

The Street, the Cyclist,
the Man Greeting the New Day

László Moholy-Nagy, *7 A.M. New Year's Morning*, Berlin, c. 1930.

The Stairs, the Grid,
the Conical Man

André Kertész, *The Old Professor*, Paris, 1928.

The Bauhaus Apartments,
the Airy Balconies,
the Commanding Tenant

László Moholy-Nagy, *Bauhaus Balconies*, Dessau, 1926.

The Pebbles, the Chairs,
the Companionable Shadows

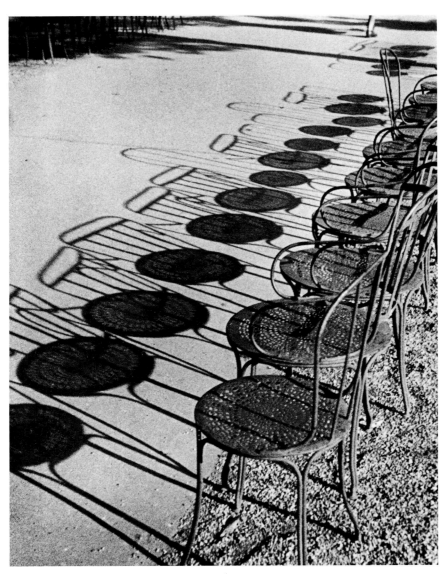

André Kertész, *Chairs of Paris*, 1929.

Same Chairs!
Different Photographer!
Aestheticism in a Rut!

Anneliese Kretschmer, *Untitled*, Paris, 1929.

The Rut

Actually, it's the entire Rutt family (the correct German spelling), in a particularly flattering shot. But this earth, photographed in Germany by Arvid Gutschow (c. 1928), is too good to be true (opposite). Nothing could possibly grow in such cultivated, unearthly ground. Photographs do lie. Whether they are still or moving pictures, "photographic reality" can of course be manipulated all too easily to establish or reinforce one line of publicity or another — line after line, one spade- and shovelful after another, producing an infinite regress of proverbial ruts.

The ruts in this picture are finally no laughing matter because they prefigure those rows upon rows of massed Nazis that would appear shortly in choreographed, geometric visions of totalitarian order, unity, force, and natural force (waves of people) such as Leni Riefenstahl's famous 1935 German film, *Triumph of the Will.* If you squint at this photo two or three times, you'll see "the waves" ripple, a mirage akin to the arresting moment in *Triumph of the Will* when a shot of SA and SS troopers massed in the Nuremberg stadium cuts suddenly to an overhead shot of hundreds or maybe thousands of rippling, undulating forms that are quite indecipherable. They could be a pack of marathon runners, or competitive swimmers, or salmon in the act of feeding or spawning, their flanks sparkling in the sun as they roll and quiver — a beautiful sight, in any event. The camera pulls back and away, revealing them as tight phalanxes of flapping flags borne by a great wedge of stationary SA members, celebratory modernism as propaganda. *The Totalitarian World Is Beautiful,* to expand Renger-Patzsch's title.

Riefenstahl managed to glorify Hitler and the party by employing arabesques, patterned shadows, sharp angles, and dramatic vantage points derived in large part from Cubism and the work of Renger-Patzsch, Moholy-Nagy, and Rodchenko (his Soviet Boy Scout [p. 105] could be from *Triumph of the Will*). The imposing early morning shadows cast by Moholy-Nagy's pedestrians and cyclist (p. 198), an emerging convention and cliché of artistic street photography, are fulsomely indulged by Riefenstahl's overhead shots of marching ranks of SS troopers who collectively cast a massive shadow, a sort of tidal wedge even more intimidating

Arvid Gutschow, *Fields*, c. 1928.

than the men themselves. Extreme low angles achieve analogous results. If the "commanding tenant" (he could be the janitor) on Moholy-Nagy's Bauhaus balcony (p. 200) were to turn to his right and thrust out his jaw, we'd have Mussolini in profile before one of his adoring Roman crowds. If he raised his right arm at a forty-five-degree angle in any direction he'd be Hitler at Nuremberg, holding his pose for at least thirty seconds while 100,000 people cheered and two dozen of Riefenstahl's strategically placed *Triumph of the Will* cameras whirred away, a great advertising crew at work. As an ad for a new building, Moholy-Nagy's Bauhaus image stresses the protuberance of the balconies and the possibility of refreshing breezes and uplifting vistas — human renewal effected by "functional" design — Bauhaus utopianism out in the open, a strong selling point. Riefenstahl's cinematic tacks in behalf of dystopia demonstrate that it's wrong to call her film a "documentary" (its frequent label) or claim that the Nazis rejected all forms of advanced art (or craft) as "degenerate."

Triumph of the Will in turn helped to establish the visual clichés of

aestheticized armed strength in America, an open-ended field first cultivated around 1940 by photographers for *Life* magazine, with low-angled
and geometrically arranged setups of real or toy military figures and aircraft — an aesthetic way of life today, war and propaganda notwithstanding. Squint at the Gutschow photo again (one slow, sustained squint, four
seconds long) and watch the earthen ridges become jetstreams in the air-
show that you recently saw in person or on television, beamed by satellite
from Great Britain, France, or a united Germany.

The ruts in question extend into contemporary living rooms everywhere, where force is aestheticized on TV and consumed by the entire
family. Perhaps even the best-educated descendants of 1940 have been
conditioned by TV's fast pace to walk too quickly through museums and
skip bookstores altogether. When a comparatively serious TV "news-
magazine" such as CBS's *Sunday Morning* surveys an art or photography
exhibition, it focuses on each work for no more than two silent seconds,
following the tempo of the "tabloid" fast takes we've just viewed. Our
balancing act of words and images challenges TV for the attention of the
masses, risking any number of ruts.

The Wheel and the Lamp

W E ' R E   O U T   O F   the rut(s), and back on track. The wheel and lamp
(p. 208) each constitutes a summarizing O — for aesthetic order, and ordinary, everyday life, with its Whitmanesque open road and democratic
pleasures such as a Sunday afternoon drive in the country or to a glittering green ballpark. We believe that this suspended lamp will work, this
tilted wheel will turn, in part because the solid, pragmatic shadow of the
wheel is level with the picture plane rather than at one more "artistic" or
arty angle that would spin away from grounded reality, an area where
subject matter counts. We should know, naturally, that this is a Model T
Ford, the low-priced car that enriched and enhanced American life in so
many ways. As photographed by the American Ralph Steiner in 1927, the
Model T's artfully framed and balanced forms are equivalent to function
and social worth. "He drove an automobile with a very fierce headlight
. . . through the darkness of this world," writes D. H. Lawrence of Whit-
man, in *Studies in Classic American Literature* (1923).

Since it's 1927, a banner year, we can imagine the great cheers that
greeted Charles Lindbergh's return to New York and the record-
breaking sixtieth home run of Babe Ruth, whose unusually heavy bat and
preeminence as pitcher and hitter when Bernard Malamud was a young
native of Brooklyn inspired the adult Malamud to create Roy Hobbs in
The Natural (1952). When Hobbs's game-winning home run smashes and
short-circuits the stadium light-towers in the 1984 film version, the slow-
motion flowering of exploding lamps against the rich, dark sky looks back
to benign Futurist salutes to technological progress such as Giacomo
Balla's famous 1909 painting *The Street Light — Study of Light* (in the Museum of Modern Art), an organically shaped "atomic blast" that celebrated the electrification that year of street lamps all across Europe.

The stylized explosions of *The Natural* represent a singular display,
since aestheticized hi-tech catastrophes in current movies and TV dra-
mas mainly affirm death and destruction, defining the fascist end of
Futurism, celebratory modernism despoiled in the form of mass entertainment, nihilism in color. In 1990, Crayola Crayons discontinued their

sunny "lemon yellow." "Too boring," they announced, replacing it with three new hues of red — better suited to explosions, no doubt, and seas of blood. Younger readers won't believe that men used to stop at urban construction sites to view buildings going up and would also drive their families out to airports such as New York's waterbound Floyd Bennett Field to watch and wave at streamlined transatlantic seaplanes taking off. Some passengers actually waved back through their portholes — that basic, not-so-abstract machine shape in Léger and Davis.

Ralph Steiner, *Ford Car*, 1927.

The Flowering Crane

LEWIS HINE'S photograph from his 1930–32 series documenting the construction of the Empire State Building presents the waving worker as a national hero, the Charles Lindbergh of American industry, whose pride, optimism, and determination should lift a democratic country out of its Great Depression. Hine's tribute to this constructive spirit looks forward to Léger's last series of monumental paintings, *The Construction Workers* of 1950 (Léger died in 1955), where "real," naturalistically depicted men (as opposed to automatons) pose casually on multicolored steel girders to celebrate nothing less than the rebuilding of postwar Europe. Of course, no art historian would gloss these paintings in so topical and journalistic a way. Conversely, Hine the reporter becomes a High Modernist, literally and figuratively, in many of his Empire State photos, a surprising shift, given the self-effacing and eye-level expository manner he had used in his earlier documentation of urban poverty and child labor. His high-flying workers could be called the progeny of the plucky little newsboys he had photographed years earlier. In the image at hand (p. 211), Hine indulges the kind of dramatic angle and vertiginous point of view associated with Moholy-Nagy and most of the other photographers we've just scanned.

Historians of photography like to categorize and confine the bravura style of these artists and artisans to a specific period — 1927–33 or 1914–39 — under epochal or art history tags (The New Vision, New Objectivity, Bauhaus) rather than see their manner for what it is, openly, even today: an easy way to elevate a subject, even if it's morally ugly or trivial; a self-reflexive call to higher consciousness (you're very aware that a *camera* is being wielded); and an injunction to us to be free-wheeling or floating camera-eyes and continue the photographer's open-minded if dizzying hunt for quotidian beauty and the "signature of all things," or William Blake's "universe in a grain of sand." Imagine Chagall, his airborne daughter, and several of his shtetl rabbis and rooftop fiddlers soaring about, armed with long-lensed Leicas. A 1928 Russian poster by the Stenberg brothers for the film *Berlin, Symphony of a Great City* incorpo-

rates a photomontage by the German photojournalist Umbo (Otto Um-
behr) that depicts a popular Berlin reporter of the day as a colossus
astride the city, sporting an actual camera for an eye as he takes in everything below, including, one can suppose, splendid flowering plants on
rooftop gardens and striking visual conjunctions on the distant ground.

The Lewis Hine who took this picture is implicitly in the position of
Umbo's colossus, extended bravely in the best tradition of adventurous
journalism. But Hine's picture also bears the imprint of the avant-garde
in art and verse, where a fragile, blooming flower in a poem may be reinforced by a spokelike ray drawn from efflorescent Futurism, Italian or
native branch:

> *From the petal's edge a line starts*
> *that being of steel*
> *infinitely fine, infinitely*
> *rigid penetrates*
> *the Milky Way*

writes William Carlos Williams in "The Rose" (1923). The symbolic
thrust of Renger-Patzsch's c. 1922 photograph of *Sempervivum percarneum* (p. 212), one of the first pictures in *The World Is Beautiful*, is
achieved by simpler means. His tight close-up crops the tips of the leaves
and makes them seem to radiate into space, toward Williams's Milky
Way, where the lighting is astral or lunar. The picture could conclude an
illustrated edition of *Ulysses* if Molly Bloom had thought solely about
flowers at the end of the book and hadn't also referred to lakes, mountains, and men.

Don Worth's photo of the so-called Succulent (*Echeveria subrigida*),
taken in California in 1976 (p. 213), echoes Renger-Patzsch, but the
strong similarities constitute a considerable difference. (Jorge Luis Borg-
es's 1939 story "Pierre Menard, the Author of the *Quixote*" rehearses the
process that allows "a copy" to be more extraordinary than the original.)
In 1928, "the world is beautiful" was an unremarkable phrase; in 1976, in
the wake of many more wars, the Holocaust, and the environmental crisis, the claim seemed fantastic or foolish — or wonderfully independent,
daring, and refreshing. This makes Worth's "derivative" picture prefer-
able to Renger-Patzsch's. Worth has managed to ride over history and
our received body of pessimism, despair, and postmodernist irony to re-

mind us of the obvious: the flowers by our backdoor still bloom each spring and summer, even as books and articles rightly warn us about the dangers of the greenhouse effect. The view from the street or our urban office window isn't necessarily bad, either.

Lewis Hine, *Empire State Building, New York City,* 1930–32.

Albert Renger-Patzsch, *Sempervivum percarneum*, c. 1922.

Don Worth, *Succulent: Echeveria Subrigida, Mill Valley, California,* 1976.

Men at Work

THUS WAS Hine's unflowery title for his 1932 published collection of Empire State Building pictures, some of which were probably influenced by Mondrian (opposite), who had a radical impact on another American, Alexander Calder, especially when the latter visited Mondrian's Paris studio for the first time in 1930. Calder was enchanted by the way Mondrian had arranged and tacked colored cardboard rectangles on one wall where another person would have displayed potted or hanging plants. "I suggested to Mondrian that perhaps it would be fun to make these rectangles oscillate," Calder later recalled, on many occasions, because the day was so important to him. Mondrian rejected the suggestion, and Calder invented the mobile.

Lewis Hine, *Empire State Building, New York City*, 1930–31.

Art History
Comes to Life

W<small>HO CAN DOUBT</small> that Hine was influenced by Mondrian, who becomes a superstructure in this context (below). Imagine that red is the sole (and soul) elevator. Hop aboard! *Thump.*

Piet Mondrian, *Composition*, 1933. 16 ¼″ × 13 ⅛″.

The New Vision

THIS COOL CUSTOMER (below) is calmly working above what Humbert Humbert would call the "friendly abyss," a characterization of deep space and moral or spiritual suspension that reverses our expectations as sophisticated students and consumers of modernism. We expect "The horror! The horror!," as Kurtz exclaims from the edge in *Heart of Darkness*, characterizing his life and death. "I had forgotten the Band-Aids," says the mock-hero of Donald Barthelme's 1970 story "The Glass Moun-

Lewis Hine, *Empire State Building, New York City*, 1930–31.

tain," as he hangs, half a mile up, on the side of the gleaming structure he is climbing in downtown Manhattan. Barthelme's story (included in his *City Life*) completely upends Hine's ethic and aesthetic, and represents postmodern nihilism and cynicism in its purest, most good-natured form. "Do today's stronger egos still need symbols?" asks the story's authorial voice. Barthelme mocks a range of possibilities, especially the symbolic idea of high altitude that I'm celebrating now. The glass mountain of the story is the world's largest example of Pop art — a block-long, mile-high Claes Oldenburg–like construct that lampoons the sublime peaks of Romantic poetry, landscape painting, and art photography, ranging from Shelley's "Mont Blanc" (1816) to Hine's high-wire workers and Ansel Adams's snow-capped High Sierras, all *blanc* (French for "white") spaces now to a word-weary postmodernist. The pun is for Joyce and Nabokov, who trusted the world more.

The affectless, ironic tacks of postmodernism are surely a product of American disillusion over Vietnam and Watergate (1965–75), though such sweeping statements represent the kind of facile certitude and cant that Barthelme sometimes satirized so well. "Postmodernism" is in any case a loose and baggy conception, except in architecture criticism. The sentence from Barthelme, however, goes a long way as a synecdoche for postmodern art, writing, photography, and popular entertainment: "Do today's stronger egos still need symbols?" Strong egos everywhere sneer at the false gods created by media publicity, and this sense of contempt can easily spread to include most everything, and then one day we find ourselves blinking with astonishment and perhaps shame at the televised spectacle of dissident Chinese students carrying a twenty-foot-high papier-mâché statue of Miss Liberty in Beijing's Tiananmen Square, and dying for it a few days later. By the end of the year 1989, as the Soviet bloc nations strived for liberty, the ordinary worker had become a hero and symbol of Eastern Europe, though David Letterman on TV continued to sustain his (postmodern?) condescension and contempt for ordinary workers and their work and aspirations. Examples could be provided, but why single out Letterman? Who in the 1980s photographed any sort of workers as though they and their work are dignified, daring, and (you're not gonna believe *this*!) worthwhile? What a concept! What a new vision!

"The New Vision" (1914–39) is new again, like Don Worth's "Renger-Patzsch," and conspicuously visible and available as an excellent 1989–91 traveling museum photo-exhibition and catalog titled *The New Vision* — a brave, new antirevisionist way to say that the past is present, a sourcebook still capable of providing a few of us with elevating symbols (towering buildings, bird's-eye views, elegant tools) that are best appreciated in the context of history. Add *The New Vision* catalog to your Twentieth-Century Celebratory Shelf, along with Raymond Carver's final collection of stories, *Cathedral* (1983). In the title story, an ordinary man watches a TV documentary about cathedrals and manages to communicate their essence to his guest, a blind man — a new vision too for Carver the recovering alcoholic. It represents quixotic, unsteady *Yes*'s victory over the castle of *No* (Steinberg's drawing, p. 63), the minimalist as maximalist. The absence of the article *the* or plural *s* on "Cathedral" marks it as a state of mind as well as an old-fashioned structure, no stained-glass mountains in sight. If the death of Stuart Davis and publication of Susan Sontag's "Notes on Camp" in 1964 mark the end of the High Modern period, then 1989, the year that Barthelme died, heralds the end of postmodernism. Coldly academic formulations are of course deathless.

On the Run

To hammer home an academic comparison of Hine and Mondrian, here is Mondrian's 1936 painting, *Composition with Blue and White* (opposite). There is nothing academic, however, about the circumstances of its composition by the cloistered modernist. The rising, columnar vertical force is powerful, but the chromatic high spirits of yellow and red have been driven away (remember the yellow of 1935? [p. 7]), undoubtedly by the dark public events of 1936, enough to mute anyone's palette and red phonograph. These events included Mussolini's successful war on Ethiopia, the fascist uprising in Spain, and Hitler's reoccupation of the Rhineland and unlawful rearming of Germany, all auguries of the vast cataclysm ahead. Fearing German air raids on Paris, Mondrian left the city after the Munich Pact in 1938, for London, where German bomb blasts would shatter the windows of his studio-apartment in 1940. Some of the pictures he painted in London are totally monochromatic. His brushstrokes, which can be as strong and definite as those of his countrymen Rembrandt and Van Gogh, are barely visible in the 47 5/8″ × 23 1/4″ *Composition with Blue and White*. His white is awfully thin — a space or altitude wanting in oxygen. (You must see Mondrian's pictures in person to discern his autographic presence.) As for us, we seem to be stuck at blue, with no red elevator in sight. We'll have to climb the rest of the way up.

Piet Mondrian, *Composition with Blue and White*, 1936.

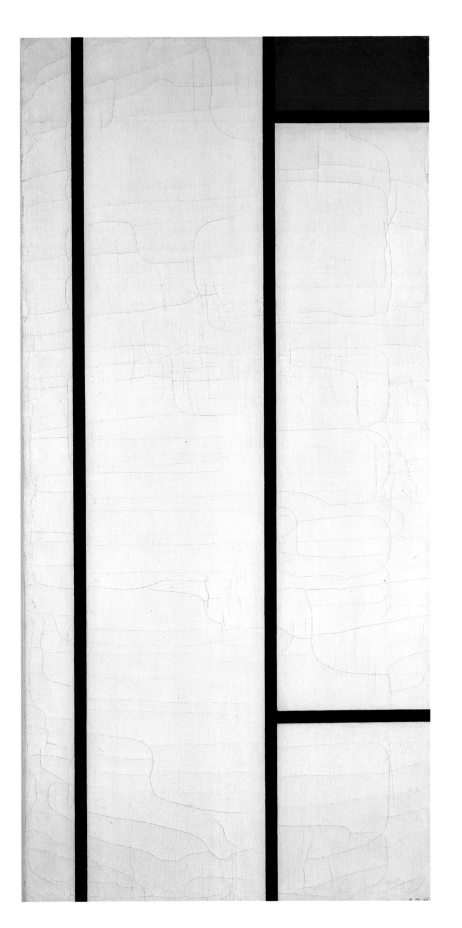

Homo Ludens

Sᴛᴇᴀᴅʏ, steady. Let's catch our breath. What's the big rush? Direct address projects the way Laurel and Hardy can still speak to us. This scene (below) is from *Liberty* (1929). Their sense of play is wisdom of a sort and serves to endorse play as a way up and out.

Oliver Hardy and Stan Laurel, in the film *Liberty*, 1929.

The Summit

THE WORKER as premier dancer and creator — choreographing, conducting, constructing, bringing the city to life — the Michelangelo of Manhattan (below). Michelangelo is evoked deliberately by Matisse in *The Dance* (p. 15), and by Yeats in "Long-Legged Fly" (1939), where a

Lewis Hine, *Empire State Building, New York City*, 1930–31.

vision of the painter, high on his Sistine scaffolding, represents the essence of the civilization that the poet would save from extinction in the oncoming war. Hine's workers are our representatives, too, if we can imagine ourselves at the edge — testing, if not mastering, such perilous heights. Imagination is *our* elevator, "A Guide to Wherever We Live." "Do today's stronger egos still need symbols?" *Yes, yes*, says one of them, Molly Bloom.

High Modern Breeze

HINE'S ULTIMATE IMAGE (opposite), the worker as *Icarus* (Hine titled him this), or a long-legged bird created by Yeats or Brancusi. Hine would have better titled his picture after Icarus's father, Daedalus, because in Greek mythology Icarus flies too high and plummets to the sea. As for Stephen Dedalus's seaside search for the "signature of all things," the looped cable in Hine's photo forms another *O*, for "overview." The pace of this final sequence, which opened with Moholy-Nagy's *View from the Berlin Radio Tower* (p. 197), tries to evoke the zing of rapid transmission, and the electricity that runs printing presses, especially the one that produced this book and this (electric?) montage—arranged and animated, I hope (if you turn the pages quickly) in the spirit of Calder's idea for Mondrian, or Calder's own achievement—*Thirteen Spines* (p. 2) in a high modern breeze. PIC-BOOK MONTAGE TOPS TWO-SECOND TV SPOTS IN RATINGS WAR declares a front-page headline in the new issue of *Variety*. UNIVERSE IS IAMBIC LINE states the *National Enquirer*. EXTRA! POSTMODERNISM KAPUT!! EXCLUSIVE PHOTOS!!! reads the front page of the New York *Post*. "Retro High Modernism: A Special Issue," promises a half-page announcement in *Art in America*.

Lewis Hine, *Icarus*, 1930–31.

Liberty

An aerial shot of the completed structure, taken from a dirigible. It was made in 1939 by André Kertész, who had been in America since 1937, on what he thought was a temporary visit (opposite). If you were Mondrian, suspended here a year later with your old Parisian friend Kertész, two refugees from Europe — suspended, then, in a figurative sense — you might have looked to the left, and seen Miss Liberty in the harbor, and then looked straight down and imagined the other gifts of the city arrayed in the following manner, as we move from this image to the next one as smoothly as the way (in Mondrian's faith) the eternal soul will one day depart from its material, mortal confines.

André Kertész, *The Empire State Building*, 1939.

It's *Broadway Boogie Woogie*, 50″ × 50″, finished by Mondrian in 1943, the same year that the young New York artist Jackson Pollock painted his nightmarish *The She-Wolf*, which was acquired by the Museum of Modern Art (in 1944), where it now shares space with *Broadway Boogie Woogie* — *Yes* squared off against *No*, to schematize once more the war in our psyche (opposite). Mondrian arrived here in 1940, to escape Hitler, at around the same time as Nabokov, Stravinsky, Auden, Chagall, Léger, Milhaud, Ernst, Lipchitz, Saul Steinberg, and numerous other European artists, writers, filmmakers, and photographers such as Moholy-Nagy (an early arrival) and John Gutmann, who quickly caught the native beat (p. 23), as did Billy Wilder. Although the seventy-year-old Mondrian was poor and in ill health (his paintings then sold for $150 each), he too responded enthusiastically to the American scene. He wandered around midtown Manhattan, especially Times Square, taking delight in the sharp brightness of its visual clutter — SMOKE CAMELS, HAVE A COKE, YANKS BOMB TOKIO; its exuberant, optimistic wartime rhythm — fleet's in, flags are up; its live jazz and dancehall performances — small groups, big bands; and the astonishing bounce of its 1940s skyline — tall buildings giving way suddenly to short ones: the eye dives down, then up again, then fifty flights down. Follow the bouncing rooftops, the zigzag course — *Swing Landscape*'s pulsating forms on the move, finally, as Astaire and Rogers dance up and down and over a stylized Art Deco landscape. "Their films represent the essence of American vitality," Mondrian had written, from Paris, in 1936. The dignified and ascetic artist, who in Europe had titled two decorous abstractions *Fox Trot A* and *Fox Trot B* (1930–31), now became an energetic if awkward jitterbug at parties and Gjon Mili's jam sessions (pp. 160–1). His new abstractions pulsated with life as never before, including his signature brushstrokes, which dart and swirl along in polyrhythmic time with the overall composition, more like bebop drumming than swing — Sid Catlett (he played every style) accompanying Charlie Parker and Dizzy Gillespie in 1943–44, the birth of the new jazz.

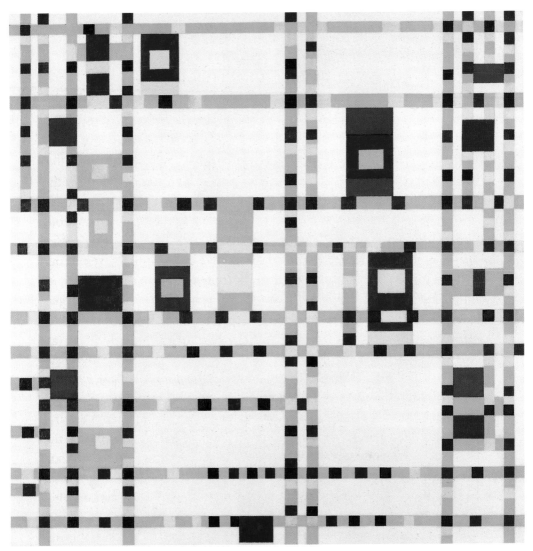

Piet Mondrian, *Broadway Boogie Woogie*, 1942–43.

Broadway Boogie Woogie, Mondrian's last completed picture — he died in 1944 — was painted while he listened to the phonograph records of the popular jazz pianists Pete Johnson, Albert Ammons, and Meade Lux Lewis (they paired variously as boogie-woogie duos), and Mondrian's great favorite, James P. Johnson, who performed frequently on "Swing Street," as it was called (Fifty-second, near Broadway), and at Gjon Mili's, his keyboard attack so powerful, recalls Teddy Wilson, that "sometimes the piano actually bounced." This picture and map, Mondrian's "Guide to New York," can still be read as a mystic's telescopic vision of the *next* world, or at least the firmament sparkling above — *The Starry Night* by

Van Gogh (1889), all angled and squared, its bursting energy rechan-neled. But *Broadway Boogie Woogie* probably moves and pleases more of us as a resilient refugee's overhead, concrete view of Manhattan at night — well, more a *conflation* of day and night, featuring clarion yellow, the fastest, loudest color we've heard in this book. Mondrian's boogie woogie "keyboard attack" compels synesthesia, evoking at once the blinking lights and neon pipelines of Times Square and Broadway, the stop and go movement of yellow cabs in heavy traffic, the piercing bleats of their impatient horns, and the jazz colors of primary rhythm instru-ments, with two pianos — James P. Johnson joining Teddy Wilson — and the drummer's headlong right hand riding the shimmering top cymbal — it's off-white and yellow — while his electric left hand hits red. *WHAM!* Blue? That's James P., syncopating on two, behind the drummer's stac-cato rim shots: *yes yes yes* in Morse code. Square viewers, fresh from Moholy-Nagy's overview of Berlin and Nabokov's Otto, will only see snow-covered rooftops — infinite space, if you imagine the multiform composition fully. *Thump. Thump. Thump. Thump.* It's old Mondrian, cautiously jitterbugging in Paradise with Henri Matisse. Because of sex-ism throughout the ages, there aren't enough women there. Those are the footsteps too of Nabokov walking between Socrates and Proust, who won't let anyone else talk. It's also the sound of the rubber-tipped cane of the narrator of "A Guide to Berlin," who lives not far from me in a very old people's home. He's walking across his little room to get another cassette from the shelf for his VCR, a Buster Keaton film from the 1920s — the one in which Buster encounters a cyclone on Main Street and just keeps on walking, leaning into the wind at a forty-five-degree angle, one hand holding his porkpie hat in place as debris whizzes by, and he keeps striding forward.

Index

Illustrations

37: Pablo Picasso, *The Race*, 1922. Musée Picasso, Paris. Copyright © 1992 ARS, NY/SPA-DEM, Paris.

41: Edward Steichen, *Brancusi in his Studio*, Paris, 1927. Collection of the author. Reprinted with the permission of Joanna T. Steichen.

45: Constantin Brancusi, *View of Brancusi's Studio*, featuring his *Bird in Space*, 1923. Musée National d'Art Moderne, Paris. Copyright © 1992 ARS, NY/ADAGP.

47: André Kertész, *Mondrian's Studio, Paris*, 1926. Copyright © 1992 Estate of André Kertész.

48: Robert Delaunay, *St-Severin, No. 3*, 1909. Solomon R. Guggenheim Museum, New York. Photograph © 1992 The Solomon R. Guggenheim Foundation. Delaunay copyright © 1992 ARS, NY/ADAGP.

49: Jacques Lipchitz, *Standing Personage*, 1916. Solomon R. Guggenheim Museum, New York. Photograph © 1992 The Solomon R. Guggenheim Foundation.

53: Marc Chagall, *Double Portrait with a Wineglass*, Musée National d'Art Moderne, Paris. Copyright © 1992 ARS, NY/ADAGP.

55: Robert Delaunay, *The Cardiff Team*, 1912–13. Musée d'Art Moderne de la Ville de Paris. Copyright © 1992 ARS, NY/ADAGP.

57: Morgan Russell, *Cosmic Synchromy*, 1913–14. Munson–Williams–Proctor Institute Museum of Art, Utica, New York.

61: George Grosz, *Funeral of the Poet Panizza*, 1917–18. Staatsgalerie, Stuttgart. Copyright © 1992 ARS, NY/Bildkunst, Bonn.

63: Saul Steinberg, untitled drawing, c. 1960. Copyright © 1960 Saul Steinberg. First published in *The New Yorker*. Courtesy of the artist.

64: André Kertész, *New York City, October 12, 1944*. Copyright © 1992 Estate of André Kertész.

67: Henri Cartier-Bresson, *Andalusia, Spain*, 1933. Magnum Photos, Inc. Copyright © Henri Cartier-Bresson.

67: Henri Cartier-Bresson, *Valencia, Spain*, 1933. Magnum Photos, Inc. Copyright © Henri Cartier-Bresson.

69: Ivan Puni, *Baths*, 1915. Collection Herman Berninger, Zurich.

71: Pablo Picasso, *Glass and Bottle of Bass*, 1914. Private Collection. Copyright © 1992 ARS, NY/SPADEM.

73: Pablo Picasso, *Landscape with Posters*, 1912. The National Museum of Art, Osaka. Copyright © 1992 ARS, NY/SPADEM.

75: Kasimir Malevich, *Lady at the Advertising Column*, 1914. Stedelijk Museum, Amsterdam.

79: Juan Gris, *Breakfast*, 1914. Collection, The Museum of Modern Art, New York. Acquired through the Lillie P. Bliss Bequest.

81: Henri Matisse, *Yellow and Blue Interior*, 1946. Musée National d'Art Moderne, Paris. Copyright © 1992 Succession Henri Matisse/ARS, NY.

83: Henri Matisse, *Portrait of the Baroness Gourgaud*, 1924. Musée National d'Art Moderne, Paris. Copyright © 1992 Succession Henri Matisse/ARS, NY.

86: Henri Matisse, page 12 of his handwritten text for *Jazz*. Paris, Teriade, 1947. Copyright © 1992 Succession Henri Matisse/ARS, NY.

87: Dmitri Kessel, Matisse modeling in clay in 1951, age eighty-two, *Life* magazine. Copyright © Time Warner Inc.

88–9: Henri Matisse, *The Circus*, plate II from *Jazz*, 1947. Collection, The Museum of Modern Art, New York. The Louis E. Stern Collection. Copyright © 1992 Succession Henri Matisse/ARS, NY.

91: Paul Klee, *Signs in Yellow*, 1937. Beyeler Collection, Basel.

96: Paul Klee, *The Little One Has a Day Off*, 1937. Collection Max Bill, Zurich.

97: Paul Klee, *Capriccio in February*, 1938. Morton G. Neumann Family Collection on loan to the National Gallery of Art, Washington.

100: Paul Klee, *Mural from the Temple of Longing* ↖ *Thither* ↗, 1924. The Metropolitan Museum of Art, New York, The Berggruen Klee Collection, 1984. All rights reserved, The Metropolitan Museum of Art.

101: Anonymous, *My Malevich*. A page from *The Post-modernism Coloring Book*, 1991. Collection of Stephen and Katherine Oshman.

103: Alexander Rodchenko, advertisement for Rezinotrest galoshes, 1923. Collection of the author.

105: Alexander Rodchenko, *Film Eye*, 1924. A poster for six films by Dziga Vertov. Collection, The Museum of Modern Art, New York. Gift of Jay Leyda.

109: Stuart Davis, *Odol*, 1924. The Crispo Collection, New York.

110: Gerald Murphy, *Razor*, 1924. Dallas Museum of Art. Foundation for the Arts Collection. Gift of the artist.

113: André Kertész, *Sécurité*, Paris, 1927. Copyright © 1992 Estate of André Kertész.

115: Walker Evans, *Shoeshine Sign in a Southern Town*, 1936. Reproduced from the Collection of the Library of Congress.

117: Walker Evans, *Signs, South Carolina*, 1936. Reproduced from the Collection of the Library of Congress.

119: Russell Lee, *Signs in Front of a Highway Tavern, Crystal City, Texas*, 1939. Reproduced from the Collection of the Library of Congress.

121: Stephen Shore, *La Brea Avenue and Beverly Boulevard, Los Angeles, California*, June 21, 1975. Courtesy of the photographer.

123: Ralph Goings, *Blue Tile with Ice Water*, 1987. Courtesy of O. K. Harris Works of Art, New York.

125: Stephen Shore, *Trail's End Restaurant, Kanab, Utah*, August 10, 1973. Courtesy of the photographer.

127: Louis Lozowick, *Still Life*, 1929. Collection, The Museum of Modern Art, New York. Gift of Abby Aldrich Rockefeller.

131: Paul Strand, *Still Life, Pear and Bowls, Twin Lakes, Connecticut*, 1916. Collection of the author.

133: Entrance Gallery, Department of Architecture and Design, Museum of Modern Art, New York, 1984. Photograph by John T. Hill.

135: "American Modern" dinnerware, glazed earthenware designed in 1937 by Russel Wright. The Brooklyn Museum. Gifts of Russel Wright, Paul F. Walter, and Andrew and Ina Feuerstein. Photograph by Schecter Lee.

137: An installation view of *Machine Art, 2*, 1934 exhibition. Collection, The Museum of Modern Art, New York.

139: Fernand Léger, *The City*, 1919. Philadelphia Museum of Art, A. E. Gallatin Collection. Copyright © 1992 ARS, NY/SPADEM.

140: Fernand Léger, pencil study for the decor of *The Creation of the World*, 1922. Collection, The Museum of Modern Art, New York. Gift of John Pratt. Copyright © 1992 ARS, NY/SPADEM.

141: Jean Hélion, *Île de France*, 1935. Tate Gallery, London. Copyright © 1992 ARS, NY/ADAGP.

142: Fernand Léger, *The Cardplayers*, 1917. Kröller-Müller Museum, Otterlo. Copyright © 1992 ARS, NY/SPADEM.

143: André Kertész, *In a Bistro, Paris*, 1927. Copyright © 1992 Estate of André Kertész.

145: Air King radio, 1935. From *Radios*, by Philip Collins, © 1987 Chronicle Books.

147: Constantin Brancusi, *The Golden Bird*, 1919. The Art Institute of Chicago; partial gift of the Arts Club of Chicago; restricted gift of various donors. Photographed © 1990, The Art Institute of Chicago. All rights reserved. Brancusi copyright © 1992 ARS, NY/ADAGP.

148: Constantin Brancusi, photograph of Fernand Léger in Brancusi's studio, c. 1922. Musée National d'Art Moderne, Paris. Copyright © 1992 ARS, NY/ADAGP.

149: Scott Burton in 1986 with granite tables and chairs he designed. Photograph by Chester Higgins, Jr. Copyright © 1985 The New York Times Company.

150: Fernand Léger, *The Three Comrades*, 1920. Stedelijk Museum, Amsterdam. Copyright © 1992 ARS, NY/SPADEM.

153: Fernand Léger, *Still Life with a Beer Mug*, 1921–22. Tate Gallery, London. Copyright © 1992 ARS, NY/SPADEM. Courtesy Art Resource.

155: Fernand Léger, Study I for *Cinematic Mural*, 1939–40. Collection, The Museum of Modern Art, New York. Given anonymously. Copyright © 1992 ARS, NY/SPADEM.

158: Stuart Davis, *Swing Landscape*, 1938. Indiana University Art Museum, Bloomington, Indiana.

160–1: Gjon Mili, jam session at his studio-loft, 1943. *Life* magazine. Copyright © Time Warner Inc.

163: Jean Arp, *Human Concretion*, 1935, 1949 cast stone version (authorized and approved by the artist). Collection, The Museum of Modern Art, New York. Purchase. Copyright © 1992 ARS, NY/Bildkunst, Bonn.

165: Joan Miró, *Landscape with Rabbit and Flower*, 1927. Australian National Gallery, Canberra. Copyright © 1992 ARS, NY/ADAGP.

167: Alexander Calder, *The Pistil*, 1931. Collection of Whitney Museum of American Art, New York. Purchase, with funds from the Howard and Jean Lipman Foundation, Inc. Photograph courtesy Perls Galleries, New York.

169: Edward Steichen, *Pear on a Plate*, 1920. International Museum of Photography, George Eastman House, Rochester. Reprinted with the permission of Joanna T. Steichen.

171: Raymond Duchamp-Villon, *The Lovers*, 1913. Collection, The Museum of Modern Art, New York. Purchase.

173: Paul Strand, *Rock, Port Lorne, Nova Scotia*, 1919. Copyright © 1971 Aperture Foundation, Inc., Paul Strand Archive.

175: Georgia O'Keeffe, *Red Cannas*, 1927. Courtesy Amon Carter Museum, Fort Worth. Copyright © 1992 Georgia O'Keeffe Foundation.

176: Edward Weston, *Nude*, 1925. Copyright © 1981 Arizona Board of Regents, Center for Creative Photography, University of Arizona.

177: Constantin Brancusi, *Torso of a Girl*, 1922. Philadelphia Museum of Art, A. E. Gallatin Collection. Copyright © 1992 ARS, NY/ADAGP.

179: Edward Weston, *Two Peppers*, 1929. Copyright © 1981 Arizona Board of Regents, Center for Creative Photography, University of Arizona.

181: Edward Weston, *Pepper*, 1930. Copyright © 1981 Arizona Board of Regents, Center for Creative Photography, University of Arizona.

182: Gaston Lachaise, *Dynamo Mother*, 1933. Collection, The Museum of Modern Art, New York. Gift of Edward M. M. Warburg. Photograph by John D. Schiff. Courtesy of Robert Schoelkopf and the Lachaise Foundation.

184: *Abstract-Schematic Idol*, Turkey, Anatolia, Early Bronze Age I–II. Beceysultan type, c. 2700 B.C. The Menil Collection, Houston. Photograph by Hickey-Robertson, Houston.

185: Alexander Calder, *Chock*, 1972. Collection of Whitney Museum of American Art. New York. Gift of the artist.

188: Gaston Lachaise, *Dynamo Mother*, 1933. Collection, The Museum of Modern Art, New York. Gift of Edward M. M. Warburg. Photograph by John D. Schiff. Courtesy of Robert Schoelkopf and the Lachaise Foundation.

191: Gaston Lachaise, *Burlesque Figure*, 1930. Fogg Art Museum, Harvard University. Photograph by John D. Schiff. Courtesy of Robert Schoelkopf and the Lachaise Foundation.

195: Louis Lozowick, *Chicago*, 1923. Courtesy of Hirschl & Adler Galleries, New York, and Middendorf Gallery, Washington.

197: László Moholy-Nagy, *View from the Berlin Radio Tower*, 1928. Collection, The Museum of Modern Art, New York. Anonymous gift.

198: László Moholy-Nagy, *7 A.M. New Year's Morning*, Berlin, c. 1930. The Metropolitan Museum of Art, Ford Motor Company Collection, Gift of Ford Motor Company and John C. Waddell, 1987. All rights reserved, The Metropolitan Museum of Art.

199: André Kertész, *The Old Professor*, Paris, 1928. Copyright © 1992 Estate of André Kertész.

200: László Moholy-Nagy, *Bauhaus Balconies*, Dessau, 1926. International Museum of Photography. George Eastman House, Rochester.

201: André Kertész, *Chairs of Paris*, 1929. Copyright © 1992 Estate of André Kertész.

203: Anneliese Kretschmer, *Untitled*, Paris, 1929. Collection of the author.

205: Arvid Gutschow, *Fields*, c. 1928. Collection of the author.

208: Ralph Steiner, *Ford Car*, 1927. Collection of the author.

211: Lewis Hine, *Empire State Building, New York City*, 1930–32. International Museum of Photography, George Eastman House, Rochester.

212: Albert Renger-Patzsch, *Sempervivum percarneum*, c. 1922. Collection of the author.

213: Don Worth, *Succulent: Echeveria Subrigida, Mill Valley, California*, 1976. Courtesy of the photographer.

215: Lewis Hine, *Empire State Building, New York City*, 1930–31. Avery Architectural and Fine Arts Library, Columbia University, New York.

216: Piet Mondrian, *Composition*, 1933. Collection, The Museum of Modern Art, New York. The Sidney and Harriet Janis Collection. Copyright © 1992 VAGA, NY.

217: Lewis Hine, *Empire State Building, New York City*, 1930–31. Avery Architectural and Fine Arts Library, Columbia University, New York.

221: Piet Mondrian, *Composition with Blue and White*, 1936. Collection, The Kunstsammlung Nordrhein–Westfalen, Düsseldorf. Copyright © 1992 VAGA, NY.

222: Oliver Hardy and Stan Laurel, in the film *Liberty*, 1929. Collection of Mona Simpson and Richard Appel.

223: Lewis Hine, *Empire State Building, New York City*, 1930–31. International Museum of Photography, George Eastman House, Rochester.

225: Lewis Hine, *Icarus*, 1930–31. International Museum of Photography, George Eastman House, Rochester.

227: André Kertész, *The Empire State Building*, 1939. Copyright © 1992 Estate of André Kertész.

229: Piet Mondrian, *Broadway Boogie Woogie*, 1942–43. Collection, The Museum of Modern Art, New York. Given anonymously. Copyright © 1992 VAGA, NY.